Dogs

Praise for Megan Rix

'If you love Michael Morpurgo, you'll enjoy this' *Sunday Express*

'A moving tale told with warmth, kindliness and lashings of good sense that lovers of Dick King-Smith will especially appreciate' *The Times*

'Every now and then a writer comes along with a unique way of storytelling. Meet Megan Rix . . . her novels are deeply moving and will strike a chord with animal lovers' *LoveReading*

'A perfect story for animal lovers and lovers of adventure stories' *Travelling Book Company*

Praise from Megan's young readers

'I never liked reading until one day I was in Waterstones and I picked up some books. One was . . . called *The Bomber Dog*. I loved it so much I couldn't put it down' Luke, 8

'I found this book amazing' Nayah, 11

'EPIC BOOK!!!' Jessica, 13

'One of my favourite books' Chloe, Year 8

MEGAN RIX is the recent winner of the Stockton and Shrewsbury Children's Book Awards, and has been shortlisted for numerous other children's book awards. She lives with her husband by a river in England. When she's not writing, she can be found walking her gorgeous dogs, Bella and Freya, who are often in the river.

Books by Megan Rix

THE BOMBER DOG

ECHO COME HOME

THE GREAT ESCAPE

THE GREAT FIRE DOGS

THE HERO PUP

THE RUNAWAYS

A SOLDIER'S FRIEND

THE VICTORY DOGS

www.meganrix.com

The Great Fire Dogs

megan rix

PUFFIN

PUFFIN BOOKS

UK | USA | Canada | Ireland | Australia
India | New Zealand | South Africa

Puffin Books is part of the Penguin Random House group of companies whose addresses can be found at global.penguinrandomhouse.com.

puffinbooks.com

Penguin Random House UK

First published 2016
002

Set in 13/20 pt Baskerville MT Std
Typeset by Jouve (UK), Milton Keynes
Printed in Great Britain by Clays Ltd, St Ives plc

A CIP catalogue record for this book is available from the British Library

ISBN: 978–0–141–36526–8

A key of fire ran all along the shore,
And lighten'd all the river with a blaze;
The waken'd tides began again to roar,
And wondering fish in shining waters gaze.

–John Dryden

RIVER THAMES
Whitehall

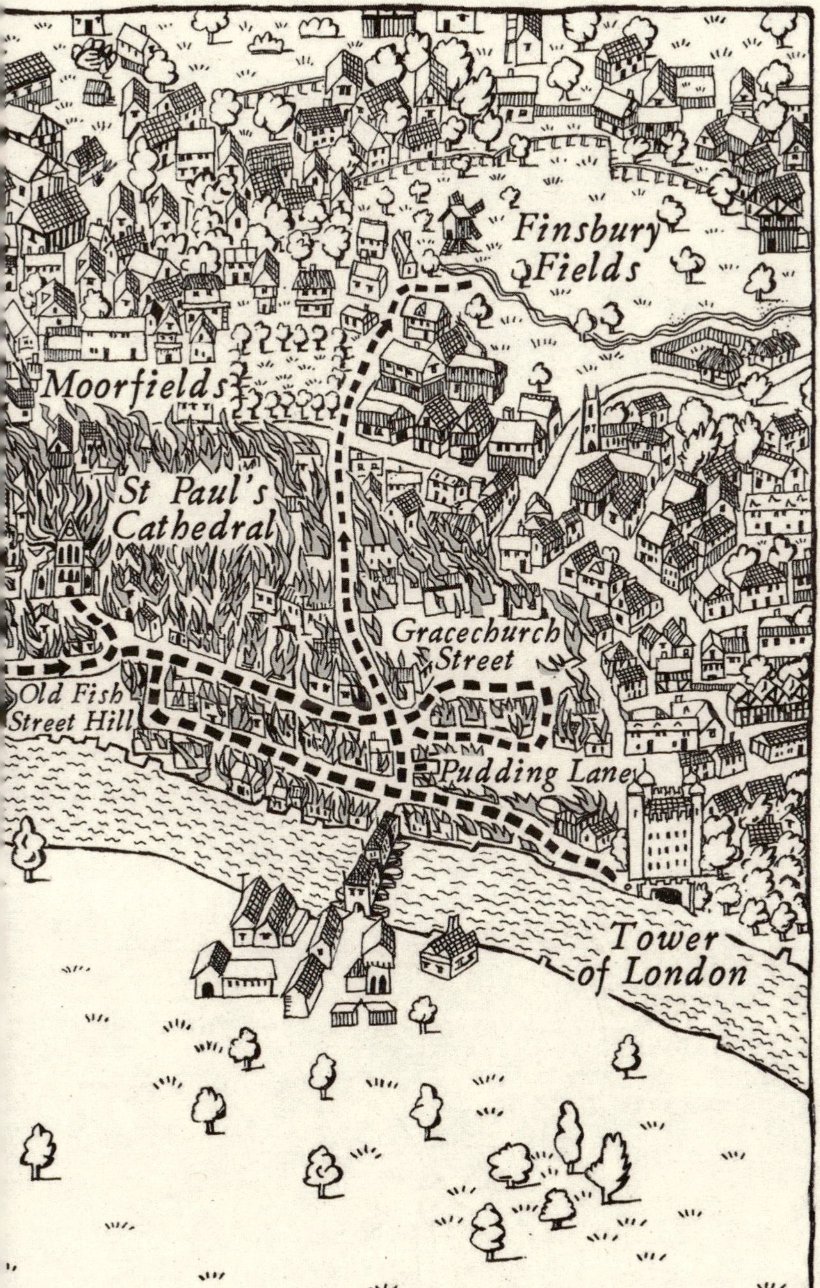
Finsbury Fields
Moorfields
St Paul's Cathedral
Gracechurch Street
Old Fish Street Hill
Pudding Lane
Tower of London

Chapter 1

February 1666

On the snow-covered south side of the River Thames, a red-faced man wearing a patched, woollen green coat and a grubby, rust-coloured waistcoat stood next to a wicker basket. Squashed inside the basket were six dock-tailed Wicklow terrier puppies.

'Wheelers – wheeler pups for sale!' the man shouted into the icy-cold air. He blew on his fingers to try and warm them up. Next to him, a man was roasting chestnuts on a fire but the dog seller couldn't afford to buy any until he'd sold a puppy. He pulled the lid off the wicker basket beside him, reached into it and grabbed the first puppy he touched by the scruff of its neck. 'These little dogs were born to work in the kitchen,' he called out to the passing people as the cream-coated puppy tried to wriggle free. 'Born to turn the cooking wheel.'

In the wicker basket, one of the puppies, the one who had been getting squashed by the first puppy's bottom, popped his head out to look at the snowy winter scene. The snow had come down hard overnight and London had woken covered in a thick white coat. There were stalls positioned all along the white banks of the river, many of them selling food. Hot pies and roast meat as well as chestnuts and gingerbread. The puppy sniffed at the delicious smells in the air and gave a whine.

'My turnspit dog got out during the plague last year and that was the last I saw of him,' a woman with an apron over her long brown skirt told the puppy seller. 'Caught by one of those awful dog catchers, no doubt.'

The puppy seller nodded. There used to be lots of dogs and cats in London's streets, most of them strays, but not any more. They were thought to carry the plague and people had been paid good money to catch and kill them.

The king's official order had been that: '*No Swine, Dogs, Cats or tame Pigeons be permitted to pass up and down in Streets, or from house to house, in places Infected.*' But the lord mayor of London had taken things a step further and ordered all stray cats and dogs to be put down, just like the last time there'd been a plague and the time before that too.

'I heard forty thousand dogs and two hundred thousand cats lost their lives,' the dog seller told the woman.

While they were talking, the puppy that had been looking out of the top of the basket scrambled free and headed off on his short puppy legs towards the frozen water's edge.

On the other side of the river, across the long bridge full of houses and shops, twelve-year-old George, palace kitchen apprentice, looked over at the skaters on the wide expanse of frozen water. Their sharp, iron-bladed skates made swishing sounds as they cut through the ice like butter. He watched in admiration as they weaved in and out of the arches under London Bridge. The bridge acted like a weir, turning the water sluggish so it was more likely to freeze. In places the ice was more than five feet thick and perfect for skating. George wished he could skate.

Some winters, when the vast Thames froze even harder than this, they held Frost Fairs on the river. Stalls were set up on the ice and people walked about on the river as if it were a street, but it wasn't frozen enough for that yet.

The small cream-coated puppy headed further out on to the ice. It was very cold beneath his tender paws and he whimpered every now and again but he didn't turn back.

'How old is it?' the woman asked, nodding at the puppy the dog seller was holding.

'Ten weeks,' the man told her.

The woman looked doubtful. 'Bit small for ten weeks old, isn't it?'

'But strong as an ox,' the man said quickly. He didn't want to lose his first potential customer of the day. 'There's more in the basket if you don't want this one. Just take a look.'

He glanced to the side of him and saw that the rest of the puppies had tipped the basket over and were making a speedy escape.

'Quick! Stop them!' the dog seller cried.

He gave the puppy he was holding to the woman wearing the apron as he ran after the escaping pups. People laughed and bumped into each other as they tried to help him scoop up the four little puppies and return them to the basket.

'Oh, look at that one,' a small girl said as a puppy ran past her. She was about to head over to him when her mother grabbed her arm.

'Don't touch it – dogs carry the plague!'

'But it's a puppy . . .' the girl said.

'The plague's over,' a man told the girl's mother. 'It must be if the king's come home.'

The bells had tolled throughout the city on the first of February for the return of the king.

'The streets are crowded with people returning to London now that he's back,' said another man.

But the woman still wouldn't let her daughter help catch the pups. She'd known too many people die from the plague to risk it. More than a hundred thousand people dead this time she'd been told and she wasn't taking any chances.

'Come on,' she said as she took her daughter by the hand and dragged her away from the riverbank.

'There should be five of them!' the puppy seller said, looking about him frantically. 'I brought six here with me today.'

But only four could be found and put back in the basket.

The woman holding the first puppy decided to buy him and handed over a few coins to the dog seller.

'You won't be disappointed,' the man told her.

The little puppy tried to wriggle away from the woman but she had it in a firm hold.

'None of that now,' she told it as they headed back across London's only bridge to the north side of the river.

From the far-off snowy north riverbank George saw something moving about in the middle of the icy river but when he looked again it wasn't there. He shielded his eyes against the bright winter sun and squinted. No, there it was again. It looked like some sort of small animal . . . but it couldn't be, could it? Maybe it was a cat. But what would a cat be doing out there? Its coat was too light for a fox.

As the puppy came closer across the ice George realized what it was and gasped. The pup looked a lot like a turnspit – one of the kitchen dogs that George looked after at the palace.

The sound of skates swishing across the ice now filled George with dread.

The skaters, all men and boys, were heading towards the puppy, faster and faster with their sharp iron-bladed skates. The puppy didn't even seem to be aware of the danger he was in.

'Look out!' George shouted, running on to the slippery ice and waving his arms about.

The puppy looked up at him and wagged his tail stub as he tried to run towards George, putting himself in a direct line with the skaters.

At the very last moment George darted forward, skidding across the ice, ripping his waistcoat and grazing his leg, but managing to scoop the puppy up as the skating group split into two around them.

'It's all right. I've got you, you're safe now,' he said to the soft furry bundle in his arms. The little puppy's heart was beating very fast but he wasn't frightened, because he had found George. His dark brown eyes looked at George and then he licked his new friend's face as the boy laughed.

'Could've been killed!' one of the skaters said angrily as they glided onwards.

'Shouldn't be out on the ice.'

'Where did you come from?' George asked the puppy when the skaters had gone. He looked around him but no one seemed to be searching for a puppy along the icy riverbank.

George didn't get much time off from his job at the palace and he'd been on his way to see his gran. His mum and dad had died of smallpox when George was five and Gran was the only family he had left. She used to work in the palace kitchen too. Humphrey the cook had given George some chicken for Gran to put in her soup, or pottage as she called it, as well as a bottle of the nasty plague-prevention water he insisted they all drank even though the plague was supposed to be over.

The old lady wouldn't want to be kept waiting.

'Looks like you're coming with me,' George told the puppy, and it licked George's face some more as they came off the frozen river and headed down the narrow cobblestoned streets to his gran's house.

Although it wasn't far it took longer than usual because there were so many people coming back to the city now that the plague had gone. So many carts and wagons were trying to get down the narrow streets that they were causing traffic jams and gridlock.

The blades of grass that had grown up around the cobblestones during the plague year, when the streets had been empty, didn't stand a chance.

George carried the puppy up Fish Street Hill where the oyster sellers were walking up and down with their baskets of shellfish.

'Cockles and mussels – who will buy?' a woman cried. 'Fresh from the sea.'

'Get your trout here,' a man called as George walked past.

The puppy sniffed at the fishy smells but he wasn't given any to try. He wriggled in the boy's arms until George set him down on the ground.

As he followed George he did his best to avoid the coarse leather boots and high-heeled, buckle-toed shoes that headed towards him, as well as the ornamental walking sticks that the men waved about as they strode forward. But more than once he gave a yelp as he was almost stepped on.

The rakers were doing their best to sweep the mess from the now slush-filled streets so people could get past. Rats followed wherever the rakers went and gorged on the rubbish piles waiting to be carted out of the city or on to the dungboats on the river.

Some people sniffed nosegays to ward off the smell. The flowers were also supposed to stop the plague's bad air from being breathed in. Wearing a dead toad round your neck was supposed to help too.

The puppy was about to sniff at a rat but George quickly scooped him up.

'We don't want you getting fleas,' he told him. 'Or being bitten. Those rats can give a nasty bite.'

They stepped to the side as a horse clipped past with a carriage behind it.

'Look out below!' a woman shouted from above as she emptied a bowl of slops out of an upstairs window.

Once Fish Street Hill had been full of cats and dogs looking for tasty morsels but not since the plague.

George didn't know how the cat that lived on his gran's roof had managed to survive without getting caught during the last year. But somehow it had.

'Raggedy Cat' as George's gran called it, on account of its ragged tail, arched its back and hissed from its spot on the roof as they turned into Black Raven Alley.

The puppy heard the hiss and looked up at the cat, his stub of a tail wagging as much as it could with George still holding him. The ragged-tailed tortoiseshell cat only hissed back.

George put the pup on the ground and he barked at the cat, then sat down in surprise as if he couldn't quite believe that such a deep, loud noise had come from him.

'Well, that was a woof and a half for a little pup,' chuckled George's gran, coming out of her front door. 'Woke me up, it did.'

The puppy licked Gran's gnarled, outstretched fingers with his little pink tongue.

'I didn't know you were getting a puppy, George,' she said.

'I wasn't until today!' George grinned.

'Is he one of the kitchen dogs?' Gran asked him.

'Not yet,' said George, 'but he'll make a perfect turnspit dog once he's older.'

'What's his name?' Gran wanted to know.

The puppy's loud bark and Gran's comment had shown George exactly what he should be called. 'I'm going to call him Woofer,' he said, running his fingers down the puppy's soft fur.

The little pup barked again and then once more, before sneezing with excitement, jumping up and moving closer to George for a reassuring cuddle.

'He is a dear little puppy,' Gran smiled. 'And I'm looking forward to hearing all about him.' She pushed open the front door.

As Woofer and George followed her, the raggedy cat hissed again.

'Has the cat let you stroke it yet?' George asked his gran.

'No,' she told him. 'Came to the door once to swallow a bit of fish, though.'

Inside Gran's rented room it was always dark because the roofs of the houses in Black Raven Alley almost touched each other and blocked out the light but George's gran didn't mind. She knew where everything was and could've found her way round with her eyes closed.

'Humphrey the cook gave me this to give to you,' George said, handing over the bottle of plague water.

Gran pulled out the cork and sniffed at it.

'What's in it?' she asked him and George did his best to remember as he ticked off the ingredients on his fingers.

'Rosemary, borage, angelica, celandine, dragonwort, feverfew, wormwood, pennyroyal, mugwort, sage and sorrel.'

'That's a lot of ingredients,' his gran said. 'But none of them should do any harm and may do some good, although I have my doubts that any of the plague waters really work.'

'Humphrey makes us drink some every day,' George said. 'Even though the plague's supposed to be over now.'

'At least he isn't making you drink anything too bad-tasting or hard to find. Do you know I heard of one plague water that has dried unicorn horn in it?'

George's mouth fell open. Where on earth was anyone going to find unicorn horn?

'I know,' Gran said. 'Ridiculous!'

Then George gave her the chicken wrapped in cheesecloth.

Gran grinned her toothless grin as she took it from him and headed over to the fire and the pottage that was gently simmering on it.

She stirred the chicken into the soup and while they waited for it to heat through George told her all about how he and Woofer had met.

'Shouldn't have gone out on the ice,' his gran scolded him. 'Too dangerous.'

'My waistcoat got torn,' George told her and showed her the tear.

Servants' clothes were provided by the palace. Different colours and types for different roles and duties. Kitchen apprentices like George had a black waistcoat, brown britches and a cream shirt.

'I'll soon have that fixed,' Gran said. 'You'll have to thread the needle for me, mind. My eyes aren't what they used to be.'

George threaded the needle and Gran set to work while Woofer sniffed at the delicious smell coming from the pot of soup on the fire.

It didn't take long for Gran to finish mending the waistcoat.

'Good as new,' she said as she handed it back to George.

'Thanks, Gran.'

'Time for some soup,' the old lady said, and she groaned as she stood up and headed to the fire.

Woofer watched as Gran ladled out a bowl of the vegetable, chicken and oat soup mixture for George and then one for herself. She put a smaller bowl of soup to cool on the side.

'Good soup, Gran,' George said as he drank his.

'Can't beat a bowl of pottage, whether it's fine weather or foul outside,' Gran agreed as she slurped hers.

Woofer whined.

'Not yet,' George told him. 'We don't want you burning your mouth.'

Once they'd eaten theirs Gran gave Woofer his bowl. George and Gran both watched, smiling, as the puppy lapped it up.

'He's very hungry,' George said.

'Starving,' she agreed.

Woofer licked the bowl clean, then sat down and gave a small whine – but no more soup came.

It was time for George to be heading back to the palace.

Gran gave him a hug.

'Thank Humphrey for me!' she called after George as she waved him and Woofer off.

The raggedy cat hissed again as they headed out of Black Raven Alley on to Fish Street Hill and along Thames Street. Woofer's sensitive nose sniffed the air. It had changed from smelling of fish to the aroma of meat now.

'This way, Woofer,' George said, and the puppy trotted after him as they turned into a street with a double row of tumbledown Tudor buildings that was too narrow for a carriage to get down. Several of the houses had a red cross painted on the door and the words LORD HAVE MERCY UPON US written on them. These were the houses where plague victims had been shut in during the last year.

'Hello there!' a voice shouted, and when George and the puppy looked up they saw thirteen-year-old Annie hanging out of an upstairs window, doing her best to clean the baker's sign. 'Be down in a minute.'

George gave Woofer a stroke while they waited.

'Hannah wanted her father's sign nice and clean, especially the bit where it says he's the king's baker,' Annie told George when she came down. Hannah was twenty-three and a baker too. She was very proud of her father.

'The sign looks good,' George said.

'Wouldn't want to go out there again, though!' Annie laughed as they went into the bakery where she worked. 'Teagh, Mr Farriner's servant, will have to do it instead.' She bent down to stroke the puppy who was looking up at her with his big brown eyes. 'Who's this little chap?'

'His name's Woofer,' George grinned and Woofer wagged his docked tail stub.

Farriner's Bakery made the hard biscuits that fed the king's navy when the sailors were at sea. It was a very important job because England was at war with the Dutch and the sailors defending the country needed feeding. Mr Farriner was always complaining to Annie that he wasn't paid quickly enough and that meant sometimes Annie didn't get paid at all. Not that she got paid much because she was only an assistant.

Annie loved baking so much she said she didn't care about getting paid. But George knew she must do really. At least she got to sleep at the baker's and was given her food there too.

Woofer sneezed at the smell of ginger coming from the shop.

'What've you been making?' George asked.

Annie's eyes lit up. 'Something new!' she told him.

'Gingerbread?' George said as he smelt the distinctive spicy aroma.

But Annie shook her head. 'Not exactly. Proper gingerbread is expensive to make and doesn't even always have ginger in it. But ginger dust is cheap and I've added a little to the sailors' hard tack. Ginger's supposed to stop you from getting seasick.'

Woofer sniffed at the biscuits cooling on the table and Annie gave two of the smaller broken pieces to George. There were lots of broken bite-sized pieces on the metal tray.

'I don't know why they cracked,' Annie said sadly.

Mr Farriner and Hannah wouldn't be pleased when they got back from the flour mill. She wasn't even supposed to be cooking. She'd been told to clean the sign and the clay oven but instead she'd been baking ginger biscuits most of the day until they were rock-hard because they might have to last for weeks or even months at sea without going stale. The broken biscuit was too solid for George but Woofer crunched his bit up and then he ate George's piece too.

'Be good for his little puppy teeth,' Annie said as they watched him gnawing away.

'I bet Teeth and Claws and Scraps would like them too,' George said.

Annie smiled as she scooped up a double handful of broken pieces for the rest of the turnspit dogs at the palace. 'Here, take a few more with you, then. I made lots.'

She hoped Mr Farriner wasn't going to be too angry with her for using the flour without asking him.

‘Thanks,’ said George as he put the biscuits in his pocket.

Woofer looked up at him meaningfully but George shook his head.

‘You can’t *still* be hungry,’ he told the little dog.

Woofer gave a puppy yap to say that he was still very hungry – but George could see his little tummy was round and full.

‘You can have some more later,’ he said, and they headed onwards down the snowy cobblestoned streets to the river.

Woofer sniffed the air again. There were so many strange and interesting smells: farm animals that had passed by on the way to market, as well as other cats and dogs and hundreds and thousands of rats. There was also the smell of rotting food – and all of it mingled with the sour stink from the river, which was used as a sewer and a rubbish tip. The icy coldness had made the stench a little less strong today but it never completely went away. A screeching gull swooped overhead and Woofer raced to catch up with George, who was a few steps ahead.

Forty minutes later they arrived at the palace.

Chapter 2

The little white and tan spaniel puppy lay on the Persian rug in the king's apartment, panting. She'd been sick on the boat coming over from France and even more sick in the coach on the way to the palace.

'She wouldn't eat or drink on the trip, Your Majesty, and when I forced her to do so . . .'

'Yes?'

'It came straight back up.'

King Charles the Second shook his head. He'd had dogs as pets his whole life and he was very worried about this little puppy, which had been sent to him by his sister Henrietta.

'She shouldn't be this listless,' he said as he opened the letter that had come with the puppy.

My dearest brother,

I'm so glad that the dreadful plague is over and you have returned to London.

I hope this little one will bring you much joy. She is such a sweet, funny (and very lively!) thing. I've been calling her Tiger Lily. She reminds me so of dear Suki who we used to play with when we were children.

Your loving sister,
Minette

'I wish my dog keeper James Jack was here,' the king said, half to himself. 'He'd know what to do for the pup but he's taken the rest of the royal dogs, even Cupid who prefers to spend his days lying on a cushion, on a hunt at Richmond.'

Outside he heard a boy's laugh and a puppy's yapping. The royal apartments were off the Stone Gallery and overlooked the Privy Garden. The king looked out of the window and saw George and Woofer playing together.

'This way,' George said as he led the puppy round the sixteen squares of grass separated by paths with a large ruined stone sundial in the middle.

Sometimes George walked slowly as Woofer followed him and sometimes he ran to keep himself warm. Woofer liked running best and he yapped with excitement as he chased after his new friend.

George was glad that there was no one else there besides him and Woofer so they had the whole garden to themselves. As usual, there was lots of courtiers' washing hanging out to dry on the walls. But now the garments were all frozen solid.

George wiggled a broken branch from a rose bush along the footpath and Woofer raced after it and pounced on it, as pleased with himself as if he'd found some long-lost treasure. When the puppy released it and went to sniff at a slug instead, George wiggled the rose branch down the path again. Woofer gave a yap and chased after it as George laughed.

'You're such a funny little puppy!' he told him.

The poorly spaniel puppy on the rug heard the happy sounds of George and Woofer playing. She slowly raised her weary head to look over at the window. She gave a soft, sad whine. Only a short while ago she'd been with her mother and her brothers and sisters playing on the lawn in France.

She was still looking towards the window when the king turned back and saw her. Now he knew what he needed to do.

His Majesty lifted the puppy up and carried her downstairs and out to the Privy Garden to join George and Woofer.

'What's your name?' he called out and George froze.

But Woofer didn't. He ran over to the man in the fine embroidered clothes and long dark curly periwig. But it wasn't the man he was interested in – it was the puppy that he was holding.

George and the rest of the kitchen staff had watched as the carriages of the king and his court rolled through the gates of the palace on the first of February, but George had been at the back and he'd never seen the king close up before, so didn't realize it was him. Although he knew by his clothes that this was a nobleman.

'George, sir,' he said.

'And what do you do in our royal palace?'

'Kitchen boy, sir, and I-I . . .'

'Spit it out,' the king said mildly.

'. . . look after the kitchen dogs.'

'Kitchen dogs?'

'Yes, sir, they turn the spits to cook the meat.'

'I once helped to roast meat,' the king said, 'or at least tried, unsuccessfully, to wind up a jack to do so.'

'Did you, sir?' asked George, amazed that a nobleman would ever have done such a lowly job. Some of the kitchens at the palace used mechanical jacks but George had never operated one. In the kitchen where he worked the dogs trotted in a wheel to turn the spit that cooked the meat. In some of the palace kitchens, men and boys turned the spits instead.

'Yes. There weren't any dogs, though, although I hear there's one or two such dogs to be found in almost every sizeable kitchen in the land. It was when I was escaping from Cromwell's soldiers and had to disguise myself as a servant. The cook was not impressed by my lack of kitchen skill and I had to excuse my clumsiness by saying that as the son of poor people we so rarely ate meat that I did not know how to use a roasting jack tool. Thank goodness the cook believed me.'

'Thank goodness,' George agreed, still not realizing who he was actually talking to.

Woofer wagged his stub of a tail as he looked up at the puppy in the king's arms.

'What do you call him?' the king asked, staring at Woofer's funny furry little face and piercing button-brown eyes.

'Woofer,' said George.

'This is Tiger Lily,' the king said as he set the puppy he was holding down on the ground. She sniffed shyly at Woofer from behind the safety of His Majesty's legs and then wagged her tail too.

The king smiled at the sight of the two puppies greeting each other.

'She's very sweet,' George said.

'But poorly,' said the king.

Tiger Lily was still not being the lively puppy that he'd have expected her to be.

'What's wrong with her?' George asked.

'Hopefully it's just *mal de mer,*' the king said, and when George looked confused he added, 'She's travelled over from France by boat and has been very seasick.'

'Oh!' George said, remembering Annie's biscuits. 'I might have just the thing to help. My friend made these for seasick sailors. May I?'

The king nodded and George offered a small bit of biscuit to Tiger Lily, who gently took it from him and ate it slowly. George offered some to Woofer, who gobbled it up and then nudged George's hand for more.

'What's in them?' the king asked.

'A little ginger dust mixed in with the flour.'

The king nodded. 'A well-known cure for seasickness.'

Both of the puppies liked the hard biscuits very much and George gave them the rest of what he had.

'I'll have to get some of those biscuits for the rest of my dogs,' King Charles said. 'The puppies certainly seem to like them.'

'Yes and they're good for their teeth too,' George said as they listened to the puppies crunching.

Now that she'd had something to eat and met a new friend Tiger Lily was feeling much better, and she and Woofer played in the garden together as George and the king watched. George tried not to shiver but he was really very cold and didn't have a coat.

The clock struck four and the king frowned as a footman headed over to them through the snow.

'Parliament awaits, Your Majesty,' the footman said.

George gulped and blushed red as it finally dawned on him that he'd actually been speaking to the king himself.

'I must away to Parliament. Take care of Tiger Lily while I'm gone, George. I'll fetch her on my return. Don't let the puppies get too cold,' the king said.

George opened his mouth but no words came out. He could only gulp and nod.

The king strode off as Woofer spotted a red squirrel and gave one of his distinctive barks as he ran over to it, closely followed by Tiger Lily. But the squirrel was far too quick for them and darted up a tree. The two puppies sat down and looked up at the creature as it taunted them from high in the branches.

George headed over to join them, still hardly able to believe that the king was trusting him to look after a royal puppy.

A few minutes later the head gardener, John Rose, came into the garden. He had three assistants with him.

Tiger Lily and Woofer ran over to say hello to John Rose and the assistants, their little tails wagging excitedly.

'Well, hello there,' John Rose said as he bent down and patted them. He raised an eyebrow at George as the assistants put their buckets of water on the path and greeted the puppies too.

'One royal and one dock-tailed?' John Rose said. Only dogs belonging to the nobility were allowed to keep their tails long. Dogs that belonged to ordinary folk, and working dogs, had their tails cut off when they were still very young. Usually the two wouldn't be playing together.

'They're just puppies,' George smiled. He felt much braver about speaking to people above him now that the king had given him such an important job to do.

John Rose nodded as Tiger Lily stood up on her back legs, put her paws on the rim of one of the buckets and had a long, long drink. Woofer went to join her and drank from the other side of the bucket, standing up on his much shorter hind legs.

The assistants started to dig into the hard ground as Woofer watched them, very interested. Digging looked like lots of fun.

'Here, puppies, what's this?' John Rose said, and he tied two strands of short rope together in the middle so that there were four ends.

Woofer and Tiger Lily both ran over excitedly and grabbed an end each with their puppy teeth while John Rose gently tugged and twisted. When he suddenly let go the puppies sat back on their bottoms in surprise. The next moment they were scrambling back up again. Now they had the rope toy and they trotted off together to play at tugging with it in the snow.

George blew on his frozen hands as Tiger Lily's long tail wagged happily and Woofer's short stub of a tail did the same. Both dogs were very pleased with their first toy.

Chapter 3

Woofer and Tiger Lily sniffed at the meaty smells as they followed George into the hot, noisy kitchen where he worked.

'What in the world have you got there?' the other kitchen staff asked as the two puppies trotted along behind him.

George grinned as he saw the startled looks on their faces.

'I knew it wasn't a good idea to let you have a day off,' said George's boss, Humphrey, laughing.

Humphrey was twenty-four years old and completely bald just like his dad, despite many, sometimes weird, attempts to regrow his hair.

He and George had become friends when Humphrey found out just how good George was with the dogs. Theirs was the only kitchen within the palace that had turnspit dogs; the rest of the palace kitchens used people or machines. The bigger kitchens had six huge meat-roasting fireplaces with long spits across each of them. Those thirty-six spits were very heavy when full of meat and could only be turned by strong men. Sometimes twelve chickens would be on the same spit at once, with other meats cooking in the same fireplace.

George had been hired as a kitchen boy and might have been a spit-turner too, or a turnbroach, as they were also called. He was glad that he'd met Humphrey and got to work with the dogs instead.

'They work much better and seem happier now,' Humphrey had said a few months after George had first been employed at the palace.

'I love working with them,' George had told him, and it was clear that the dogs loved him right back.

Tiger Lily went over to Humphrey and looked up at him with her meltingly soft brown eyes.

'Oh, my goodness,' Humphrey said. 'What an absolute sweetie.'

Woofer followed Tiger Lily over to the cook and wagged his stub of a tail.

'And I see you have a friend,' said Humphrey.

'His name's Woofer,' George said. 'And I'd like to train him as a turnspit.'

The puppy had the same long body and short legs as all the dogs who turned the kitchen wheel.

'And what about this one's name?' Humphrey asked, bending down to pat the little spaniel.

'Tiger Lily. She's the king's new puppy and she came all the way from France,' George replied.

Not much more work was done for the next ten minutes as everyone in the kitchen insisted George tell them the whole story.

'From the beginning,' said Humphrey. 'And don't leave anything out!'

While George told them how he met Woofer and then Tiger Lily, Humphrey took some chicken broth from the pot on the hearth, dipped little bits of bread in it and gently fed them to Tiger Lily. She looked very comfortable sitting in the cook's lap and being made a fuss of.

'That's it, my little poppet,' Humphrey crooned. 'This broth'll do you good.'

George was halfway through his story when a brindle-furred cross-breed dog started barking and came running over from the other side of the kitchen. Woofer went to say hello, but although the other dog sniffed at the puppy he didn't want to play. Instead he put out a paw to George and whined.

'What is it, Teeth?' George asked.

Teeth was three and he and his brother Claws took it in turns to work the turnspit wheel. The dogs were bred specially to have short legs and long bodies so they'd fit inside it. Woofer looked very much like them shape-wise but his face and colouring were different. It was more important, however, that the dogs had the right temperament to work the wheel. Some dogs hated it and would growl and bite, and no one at the palace had time to wait for a turnspit dog that didn't want to work. Other dogs were frightened by the fire, so they weren't suitable either.

Teeth ran halfway across the kitchen, looked over at George, whined, barked and then ran back to the wheel and sat beside it. His meaning couldn't have been clearer.

'How long has Claws been in there for?' George asked.

Turnspit dogs were very good at telling the time and also had a strong sense of fairness.

Claws and Teeth usually knew exactly when an hour was up and it was the other one's turn to go in the wheel.

None of the kitchen staff seemed to know how long Claws had been turning the wheel and most of them didn't much care. As far as they were concerned the turnspit dogs were called wheelers and they barely knew the difference between one dog and another. But George did. He knew the difference between all the dogs and he'd given them proper names rather than just 'Wheeler'.

He sighed loudly. It just didn't make sense to him when people overworked their animals until they got sick or injured. It seemed so pointless and cruel. The poor animal, whether it was a dog or a donkey or a horse, ended up suffering and the owner was worse off because they'd have to buy a new animal or do the job themselves!

'How long's the meat been cooking for?' he asked.

Humphrey looked over at the joint. It was more than half done.

'Few hours,' he said. 'Put it in just after you went.'

'Has Claws been turning the wheel by himself all that time?'

Humphrey looked a bit shamefaced. 'Maybe,' he said. He'd been very busy and the dog hadn't made a fuss, so he'd forgotten all about him.

'If you tire the dogs out they'll not be able to work,' George said as he headed across the kitchen to the wheel, with Woofer scampering along beside him.

An old woman wrapped in a shawl sat on a stool huddled close to the fire as people worked and milled around her. She didn't have a job as such but Old Peg had always been there for as long as anyone could remember and no one moved her away. Beside her a very old dog lay on a bed of sacking and an old blanket, fast asleep. Scraps was the oldest dog in the kitchen and had been at the palace since she was a puppy. She was a black, white and tan Welsh corgi cross and the sweetest-tempered dog George had ever met. He wished he could do something to help the turnspit dogs. He knew none of them really wanted to be in the wheels but it was better than being strays, living on the streets.

'Hello, Woofer,' Old Peg muttered and the little puppy looked up at her, his head tilted to one side.

'How's Scraps been?' George asked her, looking down at the sleeping dog beside her.

'Mostly napping, like me,' Old Peg chuckled. 'But she ate her food and drank some water too.'

George tried to use Scraps as little as possible because working the wheel was hard and tiring. But sometimes when there was a big event on and lots of meat to be cooked, he didn't have a choice, and Scraps had to help too.

Woofer looked at the dog trotting round inside the wheel with four thick spokes on it high up on the wall at the side of the fire; it wasn't that close to the flames, but it was near enough to be very hot work.

A pulley came from the wheel and was attached to the metal spit on which a joint of meat was threaded. The dog on the wall turned the wheel, the wheel turned the pulley, the pulley turned the spit and the spit turned the meat until it was cooked on all sides.

George undid one of the spokes so he could lift Claws out. The dog gave George's face a quick lick and then jumped out of his arms and on to the stone floor. Then George lifted Teeth into position instead. Now it was Claws' turn to watch his brother turn the wheel so the meat cooked evenly. If the dog stopped, the meat on the spit would end up burnt and blackened.

'In Nottingham they use geese instead of dogs to do that,' Humphrey said. 'I used to watch them when I was a boy in the kitchen at

Nottingham Castle before it was demolished and my family came to work here instead.'

Humphrey's dad ran one of the other, larger kitchens that were devoted to meat roasting and sauce making.

Tiger Lily and Woofer made little puppy growls as they tugged at the rope toy on the ground.

'Did you?' George asked Humphrey, amazed at the idea and not completely sure if he believed him.

'Yes, and I'll tell you what, they did a better job than humans or dogs.'

'Did they?' George still couldn't quite imagine it.

Humphrey nodded. 'Geese can keep going for much longer, sometimes as long as twelve hours. There's lots of things geese can do besides filling up a person's tummy.'

'Like what?' asked a kitchen apprentice who was chopping onions.

'Well, they can keep watch better than a guard dog for a start.'

George shook his head.

'It's true,' Humphrey insisted. 'Their eyesight is much better than a person's or a dog's for that matter.'

Tiger Lily had had enough of playing with the rope toy and headed over to Old Peg and Scraps to say hello.

'Hello, little princess,' Old Peg said.

Scraps half lifted her head and made a soft sound.

After she'd let the old woman stroke her, Tiger Lily curled up next to Scraps and went to sleep. The old dog gave the puppy a lick on her furry head. She didn't go back to sleep again but lay there watching the puppy.

'Woofer won't be ready to work the wheel for a good few months yet,' George said to Humphrey.

'Well, he can help keep the rats down until then,' said Humphrey.

Rats were everywhere and Humphrey had had a nasty shock one morning when he'd woken up to find one asleep on his bald head. He'd been dreaming that his hair had finally grown back. Rats could give you a nasty nip too, worse than any flea bite.

Teeth and Claws were both very good at rat-catching, corralling them until it was too late for the creatures to escape.

'Anything that helps to keep the rats out of the kitchen is good with me,' Humphrey said.

Tiger Lily and Woofer were fast asleep next to Scraps after their busy day when a man wearing long boots and a footman's uniform came into the kitchen. He was holding a thick warm coat in his arms.

'I'm James Jack, keeper of the royal dogs,' he said. 'I've been hearing all about our new puppy and a kitchen boy called George who helped her get over her seasickness.'

'I'm George,' George said shyly.

James Jack nodded. 'The king thought you could use this,' he said, holding out the coat.

'Th-thanks,' George said. He couldn't believe his luck. He'd never had such a fine coat before.

'His Majesty mentioned something about you having a supply of biscuits made for dogs?'

George gulped. He hoped he wasn't landing Annie in trouble but the dogs had loved her biscuits. 'That was my friend Annie,' he said.

'Smart girl,' James Jack said.

'And a great cook,' said George.

'Well, the king wants you to buy some more from her, enough to last a few weeks,' James Jack said, and he gave George some coins to pay for them.

George looked down at the money. It was more than he or Annie, or both of them put together, earnt in a week.

'Come on now, little one,' James Jack said as he gently lifted Tiger Lily from the floor. The little spaniel looked up at him and gave a giant puppy yawn.

Woofer rolled on to his back with his legs up in the air and opened his eyes.

When he saw Tiger Lily being carried away he scrambled up and gave a woof as he ran after his friend.

'Don't worry, you can play with her again soon,' James Jack told the puppy as he and Tiger Lily left the kitchen.

'Come back, Woofer,' George called to him, waving the rope toy. Woofer stopped and looked back at George. Then he looked back at where Tiger Lily had gone and whined.

Chapter 4

The king and the rest of his dogs were waiting for Tiger Lily in the royal apartments.

'Here she is,' James Jack said as he carried her in.

Tiger Lily looked back at the door behind her and the stairs they'd just come up. Down the stairs was the kitchen. In the kitchen was her friend Woofer.

'And looking much healthier than when she first arrived, I'm pleased to say,' said the king as James Jack set the puppy down on the Persian carpet.

Tiger Lily went to sniff and put out her paw to a black and tan spaniel with a greying muzzle.

'That's Cupid,' the king told Tiger Lily. 'He was at my coronation.'

Cupid was lying on his cushion after a long day out in the cold snow. He was tired and he didn't want to play with a puppy. He told her so once with a grumble, and a second time by moving off his cushion away from her. But Tiger Lily just followed and tried to climb on him to get him to play. This time Cupid let out a loud, angry growl and Tiger Lily gave a squeal and ran away to hide under the bed.

'Now then,' said James Jack, kneeling down and stroking the frightened puppy when she was brave enough to poke her head out. 'You should know better than to mither an old dog when he's tuckered out.'

He picked her up and set her down on a soft velvet cushion.

Tiger Lily was so tired she could barely keep her eyes open and soon fell fast asleep as he stroked her.

But sometime during the night she woke up and crawled off her cushion to lie by the door that led back to her friend. And as soon as the door was opened the next morning by the woman who'd come to fetch the chamber pots, Tiger Lily slipped out unseen.

She stopped at the flight of stairs. The steps looked huge and it was such a long way down, but she was determined and so she half hopped, half fell, and sometimes needed to sit down and steel herself. Finally she made it all the way to the bottom and scampered into the kitchen to find her friend.

Woofer had been sleeping on top of George on his wooden pallet bed but even before Tiger

Lily was through the kitchen door he was up and running over to her.

Humphrey was busily making the plague-prevention water for the day. It might have almost come to an end in London but the plague was spreading outside the city and he wasn't taking any chances.

He'd already put a mashed parsley and garlic paste on his bald head in the hope that it would help his hair regrow.

'You'll have to take her back to the king's apartments,' Humphrey told George when the puppies had had a play and a bit of chicken for breakfast. 'Creep in, though, and don't let anyone see you. Don't worry, His Majesty will still be sleeping.'

'But what if someone does see me?' George said.

He'd never been in the royal apartments before and he was worried he might get into trouble.

'They won't. Now hurry up before the king wakes.'

George picked up Tiger Lily, who gave his face a lick with her little pink tongue.

'You stay here, Woofer,' George said.

But Woofer had no intention of doing that. Going up the stairs was easier than coming down them, in spite of his short legs, especially when he had George and Tiger Lily to follow.

George did his best to creep into the king's rooms as quietly as he could.

'You wait there, Woofer,' he said.

But Woofer wagged his tail and ran past George to join Tiger Lily. The two of them scampered through the open door of the king's anteroom together.

George crept in after them. He could hear snoring coming from the royal bedchamber.

'Woofer,' he hissed. 'Woofer – come back. Tiger Lily!'

But the puppies didn't return. The legs of the king's huge bed held it just high enough for a puppy to crawl comfortably beneath the mattress frame. Under the bed there were lots of interesting smells to sniff at as well as a few old bits of food to taste.

George peered round the door. He could see a lump in the bed but no puppies.

'Woofer? Tiger Lily?' he whispered.

From under the mattress he heard a puppy sneeze.

'*Woofer!*'

George crouched down and looked in the direction of the sneeze while the body lying in the bed continued to snore.

'*Woofer – come out!*' He stretched an arm as far as he could under the bed to try and reach the dog but Woofer and Tiger Lily squirmed away to the other side. George crept round to try and reach them from there but the mischievous pups crawled away again on their tummies.

As George's hand wiggled about in different directions the two puppies really began to enjoy the game, scuttling back and forth, faster and faster, until they came out from under the bed so quickly that they bumped into a wooden stand on which hung a long black curly wig that came tumbling down and landed on top of Woofer. He started to wrestle it with his teeth and shook it from side to side making growling sounds. Then Tiger Lily started to pull at it from the other side.

'*No, Woofer, no! Please stop!*' George cried as the sleeper awoke and started to laugh when he saw what the puppies were doing.

'That's it, little Tiger Lily – you defend His Majesty from that violent beast,' the king said.

George barely recognized the king with his closely cropped hair.

Woofer caught sight of another dog in the room and promptly let go of the prize, leaving Tiger Lily holding the wig in her teeth, looking up at the king and wagging her tail.

She'd seen herself in a mirror before. But Woofer had never seen a reflection of himself and he did a double take when he saw the shaggy-coated dog to the side of him. When he turned his head to have a proper look, the other dog turned its head too and looked straight back at him, bold as brass!

Tiger Lily tried to climb on to the king's bed and he lifted her up so she could nestle herself among the soft feather pillows and be stroked.

'He's not the most handsome of dogs but there's something endearing about his funny, furry little face,' said the king, looking at Woofer. Woofer wagged his tail as if he were agreeing – and the dog in the mirror wagged his tail too.

When George tried to grab him, Woofer quickly dived back under the bed.

'I'm sorry, Your Majesty,' George said as he stretched out an arm to grab hold of Woofer.

But the king didn't mind at all. 'Tiger Lily does seem to have taken to you,' he said.

'And I to her, sir,' said George.

'I can't wait to tell James Jack all about it when he returns with the rest of the dogs from their morning walk.' The king smiled as George carried Woofer out of the room and back down to the kitchen.

Almost every day throughout the rest of February and March Woofer was sent for to play with Tiger Lily. Or else she found her own way to the kitchen.

The two puppies grew and grew and George went twice more to buy biscuits from Annie for them and the rest of the royal dogs.

Gran was pleased when he stopped to visit her on the way and Humphrey always sent something tasty with George for her to put in her soup. Nevertheless, George didn't like how frail his gran was looking.

Annie had hardly been able to believe it when George had told her that the king wanted her to make biscuits for the royal dogs.

'One of your kitchen *experiments* finally worked,' Hannah Farriner said.

Annie blushed red. His Majesty had given his approval of her cooking. Now she was the king's baker too or at least the king's dogs' baker.

'It's all very well wanting Annie to make more biscuits but where's the money to pay for them?' Mr Farriner said gruffly.

The sight of the coins the king had given George put Mr Farriner in a much better mood and he immediately forgave Annie for her kitchen experiments.

'Maybe we should all start making dog biscuits,' Hannah joked.

Every night when George lay down on his wooden pallet bed in the kitchen, Teeth, Claws and Scraps slept close to him. Woofer usually nestled on his chest with his head pressed under George's chin.

'Extra warmth,' Humphrey laughed, 'and the fleas'll jump on them instead of you!' But the fleas still bit George, as they bit everyone.

Late one April night, when Woofer couldn't get to sleep, he gave George's face a lick. George was finding it hard to sleep too because of the heat of the kitchen. Teeth, Claws and Scraps looked at him as they panted.

As soon as George stood up, the dogs followed him out into the Privy Garden.

George kept a watchful eye as the animals sniffed and played together, not completely sure that they were really allowed there.

Scraps was having a long drink from the ornamental fountain, and Teeth and Claws were playing as usual, racing round and round the garden in a joyful game of chase. George looked around for Woofer but he didn't want to call out his name for fear of waking anyone, especially the king, in the buildings that overlooked the garden. So he hissed instead.

'*Woofer!* Woofer – where are you?'

A dog's hearing is so good he was sure that Woofer could hear him. But whether he came or not depended on how Woofer was feeling.

Upstairs in the king's bedroom, Tiger Lily watched the kitchen dogs playing under the starry, moonlit sky from the window.

She wanted to be outside too and gave a whine as she saw George running towards Woofer, who was half hidden by a bush.

From the king's bed behind her there came a loud snore.

Tiger Lily gave a sigh and rested her head on her paws.

'*Woofer,*' George hissed when he saw what the dog was doing. '*Stop that!*'

Woofer had dug down so far that only his wagging stub of a tail could now be seen.

At the sound of George's voice Woofer emerged from the hole he'd been digging. His snout was covered in soil and his pebble-brown eyes were shining.

'Look, I know you're having fun . . .'

Woofer's tail stub wagged his agreement.

'But you can't dig up the royal pineapple!' George did his best to stuff the rotted fruit with the small white roots back into the hole from which it had been pulled, and then patted the earth down.

Woofer watched him patiently and then once George had finished he started to dig the pineapple up again.

'No, Woofer!'

It was time to head back inside.

'Come on!'

Woofer looked up at the window where His Majesty now stood beside Tiger Lily. George looked up too and the king raised his hand in a wave.

Woofer wagged his tail-stub at Tiger Lily and gave one of his distinctive deep barks before following George, Scraps, Teeth and Claws back inside.

Chapter 5

Spring 1666

Tiger Lily and Woofer were both such clever puppies that in no time at all they'd learnt how to 'sit', 'stay', 'down', 'circle' and walk backwards on command.

George used only the tiniest morsels of cheese during training, or a broken bit of one of Annie's biscuits, because he knew too much rich food wasn't good for a puppy's sensitive tummy.

'Sit,' George said to Woofer, and as he said the word he lifted the hand containing the tiny bit of cheese up to his chest.

Still intently watching the hand with the cheese in it, Woofer did so. Like the rest of his breed, when he sat, his entire body was vertical with his hind legs sticking straight out in front of him.

'Good dog!' said George, and he gave Woofer the morsel of cheese.

Tiger Lily watched him and then looked up at George.

'Your turn now, Tiger Lily.'

Tiger Lily's tail wagged. Learning was fun.

George repeated the command, along with the hand signal, and Tiger Lily immediately sat.

When the king saw all the new things that Tiger Lily had been taught he was very impressed.

'She's learnt far more than my other dogs at her age,' he said as he watched her circling one way and then the other. 'It's almost as if she's dancing. What a clever puppy you are, Tiger Lily.'

The next time he saw the puppies learning new things he said: 'They should perform at the May Day celebration so the rest of the court can see what clever pups they are.'

George gulped. The idea terrified him but he couldn't say no to the king.

The following day a dulcimer and a musician to play the instrument was provided for the puppies to 'dance' to and for the next few weeks Woofer and Tiger Lily practised every day until George only needed to give them the subtlest of hand signals and no voice command at all for a perfect performance.

'Costumes!' His Majesty said when he saw how well Tiger Lily and Woofer were doing. 'Bejewelled collars for them both.'

And the royal costumier set to work.

'You're probably the only turnspit dog in history to have worn a collar embedded with sapphires,' George told Woofer when he tried the puppy's new collar on.

He'd have to be very careful that Woofer didn't lose it, and that he kept it clean, despite being a dog who loved getting grubby. When the tide was low George sometimes took the puppies out of the door at the back of the king's apartments and along the riverbank. Both Woofer and Tiger Lily loved racing and chasing each other along it. But they always got covered in grey mud, especially Woofer, who couldn't resist digging in it, and George had to give both puppies a bath before he returned Tiger Lily to the king.

The palace kitchens were even busier than usual as they got ready for the May Day celebrations. But busiest of all were the gingerbread makers in the kitchen next to George's. Master Vogel, who'd come all the way from Austria, could often be heard shouting at one hapless assistant or another.

George was glad he worked in Humphrey's kitchen. There you were more likely to hear Humphrey's big belly laugh than any shouting.

George both admired and was intrigued by the intricate work of the gingerbread makers. He knew that Annie would be really interested to hear all about it.

But Master Vogel was not pleased when George tried to take a closer look.

'Get back to your own kitchen and take that filthy diseased mutt with you!' he said.

George looked down at Woofer who'd followed him and then up at Master Vogel in disbelief. The puppy wasn't filthy or disease-ridden. Woofer looked up at George and wagged his tail-stub.

'*Now!* I don't want its fleas or a stray strand of dog fur damaging my work,' the chef told him.

Master Vogel was one of those at the palace who'd said that the turnspit dogs should be put down during the plague. Thank goodness

Humphrey had been able to overrule him and the dogs were allowed to stay.

'Come on, Woofer,' George said, and they headed back to their own kitchen.

Far fewer people were dying from the plague now in London but it hadn't completely gone. No one was absolutely safe and it was still taking lives in the rest of the country. One village in Derbyshire, Eyam, had decided to quarantine itself when plague had struck, so that it wouldn't spread the disease any further.

Humphrey still insisted his kitchen staff drank his plague-prevention mixture every morning, just in case.

'I don't care what it tastes like, it's better than getting the plague,' he declared firmly to everyone who worked in the kitchen.

George drank the contents of his beaker but it was hard to take Humphrey seriously because of the crushed acorns and honey mixture on top of his bald head.

Woofer was very fond of honey and tried to lick some of it off Humphrey's head when he bent over to pour Old Peg a beaker of plague water.

'Leave my hair restorer alone, dog!' Humphrey told him as George grinned.

The celebration of May Day had been forbidden during Oliver Cromwell's rule but with the restoration of the king in 1660 it had been reinstated.

In the morning the king promenaded through Hyde Park with his courtiers, all dressed in green with flower wreaths on their heads. There were maypole dancing and morris men and a May queen was crowned to celebrate the first of May and the first day of summer.

Woofer watched as Teeth and Claws took it in turns to walk in the turnspit wheel to cook the meat. Hundreds of people needed to be fed and all the palace kitchens were working as hard and fast as they could.

Master Vogel shouted at his assistants as they iced the hundreds of hawthorn-shaped gingerbread flowers with white icing.

The Stone Gallery was decorated with freshly cut, sweet-smelling May hawthorn blossoms from the gardens.

'It's magical,' George said. He'd never seen anything so beautiful before. Woofer barked in agreement.

A long table had already been set and George couldn't believe how much food was laid out on it. Master Vogel's gingerbread-flower display was the centrepiece of the royal table.

At three o'clock James Jack brought Tiger Lily into the gallery, wearing her ruby-studded collar.

'And now for your delight,' the king announced to the assembled courtiers and guests, a strange little smile on his face, 'may I present Miss Tiger Lily and Woofer.'

The king nodded to the dulcimer player and the musician struck the strings with sticks that were hard on one side and soft on the other.

Tiger Lily and Woofer stretched out a paw to each other as if they were saying hello. Then they circled to the right and then the left, gave a play-bow and stepped back and forward, before repeating the dance. They performed perfectly and at the end of the dog dance everyone clapped and clapped.

George was hidden behind a screen and felt as proud as could be of the two puppies. James Jack slapped him on the back

'You're a natural-born dog trainer!' he said.

George wished his gran could have seen the performance. Now it was over he was looking forward to telling her all about it.

He headed over to Tiger Lily and Woofer as the king fed them each a gingerbread flower from the display in front of him.

Woofer liked his so much that he sat down in his distinctive sitting pose and put out his paw to the king for another. His Majesty laughed and gave him a second and a third.

George took Woofer back to the kitchen while Tiger Lily hopped up on to the king's lap.

'How did it go?' Humphrey asked and George grinned. It couldn't have gone better.

Shortly afterwards Master Vogel's gingerbread display, or at least what was left of it, was brought out to the kitchen with a message from the king that it was for Woofer and his friends.

'Delicious,' said Humphrey, stuffing three whole flowers into his mouth at once.

George tasted one. 'Mmm, Gran would love this – and so would Annie.'

'Put some in your pocket for them then,' said Humphrey. 'They're Woofer's friends too.'

George had only just done so when a furious Master Vogel came into the kitchen. His face was bright red and he was very angry. The kitchen, which had been very noisy only a moment before, suddenly went silent.

'I didn't make this masterpiece for you or the kitchen dogs to eat!' the chef shouted, and he lifted up the silver platter and smashed the beautiful gingerbread display on the floor.

Then Master Vogel stormed off as Woofer, Teeth, Claws and Scraps licked up the mess he'd made.

Humphrey rolled his eyes at George and said, 'Bet you're glad you're working in my kitchen and not his!'

George nodded as everyone started talking again.

Early the next morning Woofer, Teeth, Claws and George headed out of the palace with some of the gingerbread flowers that Woofer had earned, together with some meat and bread that Humphrey had given them.

Scraps didn't go with them because George was worried that the long walk would be too much for the elderly dog. So she stayed next to the fire with Old Peg instead.

George had never taken Teeth or Claws to visit Gran before but he was sure she'd like to meet them.

The two dogs sniffed at the different food smells coming from the streets as they followed Woofer, who was leading the way.

George wished Gran could have seen Woofer's beautiful sapphire-studded collar but he'd returned it to the royal costumier after the May Day performance.

The puppy led Teeth and Claws down Red Chick Lane, famous for its chickens, along Fish Street Hill and then into Black Raven Alley where George's grandmother lived.

The raggedy cat was on the roof as usual. But this time, before it had a chance to hiss, Woofer gave a quick, friendly woof and wagged his tail-stub as if he were saying hello. He knew the creature was all hiss and no bite. Teeth and Claws, however, weren't so sure about the cat and looked the other way, pretending they couldn't see it.

As soon as George lifted the latch to Gran's front door, Woofer bounded in front of him, and Teeth and Claws followed them both into the small dark room. Woofer drooled at the delicious smell of pottage gently cooking on the fire.

'Gran?' George said as Woofer stopped in front of the old lady, asleep in her chair. 'Gran, are you OK?'

At a lick on her hand from Woofer, George's grandmother shuddered and woke up. She blinked at the dog standing before her, eager to be patted, as if for a moment she wasn't quite sure who he was. But then she said, 'Well, hello there, Woofer. My how you've grown from that little puppy I first met.'

Then she saw George with Teeth and Claws and smiled a wide, toothless smile.

'George, I was just dreaming about you,' she said as she clasped his hand with her bony fingers.

She looked even thinner than the last time he'd been here. George bit his bottom lip.

'I should have come before,' he said.

'What? No, of course not,' she said, groaning as she stood up and headed over to the pottage simmering on the fire. 'I'm fine. You know me. Tough as old boots.'

George smiled. He wished Gran *was* as tough as old boots but he knew she wasn't. She was looking frail.

Teeth and Claws shyly came forward to be stroked by Gran as Woofer tilted back his head to sniff once again the delicious smell of soup, whining hungrily.

'What have you got in it?' George asked as his gran gave the pottage a stir.

'Oats, two carrots, a radish and some herbs,' she told him.

'Might like to add this to it then,' George said as he took from his waistcoat pocket the wrapped-up bit of beef Humphrey had given him for her.

'Yes, I would,' she said, smiling, and she tore the beef up into small pieces and added it to the pot on the fire.

'Plus some bread,' said George, reaching into his other waistcoat pocket. The bread was baked at the palace and much better than most you could buy from the street sellers. Gran had found a stone in one loaf she'd bought.

'And there's this to try. It's a present from Woofer really,' George said, giving her one of the delicate gingerbread flowers.

'Almost too beautiful to eat,' she said as she took the smallest of bites from the gingerbread flower. Then she pulled a face. 'Bit rich for me,' she decided. 'Think I'll stick to my soup.'

Teeth and Claws lay down in front of the fire. Woofer looked at George's gran meaningfully and then back at the soup but she only shook her head. 'You can have some when we all do,' she said. 'The beef hasn't had a chance to flavour it yet.'

While they waited George told her about all the food at the May Day celebration and Woofer and Tiger Lily's dance.

'You should have seen her, Gran, she's such a good dog.'

Woofer gave a whine and George stroked him.

'And you're a good dog too,' he laughed. 'In fact you're even better.'

Woofer made a funny little noise that sounded almost as though he were agreeing with him.

Then Gran divided out the soup, but George couldn't help noticing that as she did so, she winced as if she were in pain and held her stomach. Woofer sat up very straight and offered his paw but she wouldn't let the dogs have their portions until it was quite cool.

'I'll come back to visit as soon as I can,' George said when it was time to go.

'You're a good lad,' she told him. 'Your mum and dad would have been proud of you.'

George worried about Gran on the short walk to Pudding Lane, and Woofer stayed close, looking up at him with his head tilted to one side every now and again, as Teeth and Claws trotted along behind them.

Annie was very excited about the gingerbread flower that George brought for her to try.

'Mmm,' she said, breaking off a delicate petal and closing her eyes to concentrate on the taste as she popped it into her mouth. 'Almonds, and ginger, but not ginger dust – proper root ginger and sliced fine as a hair's breadth, aniseed definitely and maybe just a spoonful or two of rosewater and just a hint of tansy. It really is very, very good, George.

Well done, Woofer, for earning something so delicious.'

Woofer wagged his tail at the sound of his name but he was really more interested in joining Teeth and Claws as they sniffed at the mouse family that lived under the oven.

Hannah came into the kitchen to say hello but when George gave her one of the gingerbread flowers she decided not to eat it.

'It's too pretty for that. I'm going to keep it instead,' she told him.

'More dogs than people in this kitchen!' Mr Farriner complained, coming in a few moments later. 'My customers won't be able to buy bread.'

'We'd better be getting back,' George said hurriedly, once he'd given the baker a gingerbread flower too.

Annie came with him to the corner of Pudding Lane.

'I'm worried about Gran,' George admitted. 'She hasn't been right for ages.'

'I'll pop round and keep an eye on her when I can,' Annie promised.

'Thanks. Come on, dogs,' George said, and Woofer, Teeth and Claws trotted along beside him as they all headed back to the palace.

Chapter 6

As the dry spring turned into an even dryer summer London grew hotter and the palace kitchen became almost unbearable. George, Woofer, Teeth, Claws and Scraps headed out of it through the early morning mist just after four o'clock on the last day of July.

Woofer, Claws and Teeth never seemed to tire of playing. Scraps, however, got very weary and now often chose to stay indoors when the others went out to play. But today she staggered to her feet, wagged her tail and came along too.

Woofer's current favourite place to play was St James's Park. Although still part of the palace grounds it was much, much larger than the Privy Garden and had lakes, squirrels, foxes, bats, ducks, swans and even two great white pelicans that had been given to the king and lived on Duck Island. The shallow water around it was just perfect for the pelicans and perfect for Teeth and Claws to cool off in too. George removed his shoes and waded in after the two dogs. The water was lovely and cool. Scraps paddled at the side with Woofer.

'Come on, Woofer!' George called to him. 'Come and have a swim.'

But Woofer was frightened of the water and didn't go in further than his paws and barked at Teeth and Claws, warning them to come out when they swam off.

Woofer wasn't too sure about the pelicans either, and he was very scared when one of them waddled over the grass towards him and opened its giant beak. Woofer headed off to a safe spot behind a tree until the pelican went back into the lake.

He wasn't scared of the red squirrels in the trees, though, and spent a lot of time barking and chasing after them. Not that the squirrels were worried as they jumped from branch to branch, almost laughing at the dog with the short legs and long body who thought he could catch one of them.

It was almost six o'clock by the time George, Woofer, Teeth, Claws and Scraps headed back through the park to the palace. It was far later than George had intended but he hoped Humphrey wouldn't mind. The dogs, Teeth and Claws at least, had worked hard the day before. Woofer had not worked so hard. In fact he'd run off when George wanted him to have a try at walking in the spit wheel.

'What's going on?' George asked when they arrived back.

Servants were loading goods into coaches and carriages.

'The queen's taking the waters at Tunbridge and the king's going with her and that means just about everyone else at Court is going too!' he was told.

'Are we going?' George asked Humphrey.

Lots of the kitchen staff would be required to feed the members of Court while they were in Tunbridge.

But Humphrey shook his bald head, which was covered in a thick layer of ginger-spice paste today.

'We're one of the few that aren't needed,' he sighed. It would have been nice to get out of London and into the countryside for a bit.

Once the servants had set off to get everything ready for them, the king and queen and all the courtiers prepared to leave too.

Tiger Lily came into the kitchen to see her friend Woofer, as she did every morning. Her long feathery tail wagged happily and Woofer's tail-stub wagged back just as quickly as the two puppies sniffed each other's faces.

The next moment Tiger Lily let out a squeak of surprise as James Jack lifted her up.

'There you are,' he said. 'The king's been waiting for you!'

Woofer ran after Tiger Lily as James Jack carried her out of the kitchen.

'No, Woofer,' said George, but Woofer didn't listen to him. He wanted to be with his friend.

Tiger Lily wriggled in James Jack's arms, wanting to be with Woofer.

Woofer gave one of his distinctive barks as George ran up to them.

'OK, you can say goodbye,' James Jack said, putting Tiger Lily down for a second.

As soon as she was on the ground Tiger Lily ran to Woofer and licked his face. George gave her a stroke. He was going to miss the little spaniel while she was gone.

'His Majesty's waiting,' James Jack said, and George nodded.

'Back to the kitchen, Woofer,' he commanded firmly and Woofer followed him as Tiger Lily looked after her friend, whining as James Jack carried her out to the waiting carriages.

She wasn't at all happy to be separated from Woofer. Even being the only one of the king's dogs allowed in the royal coach and being petted and stroked by His Majesty didn't cheer her up.

'You'll soon forget all about the kitchen dog when we reach Tunbridge,' the king told her.

Tiger Lily gave a big sigh as she looked out of the window. There were horses and coaches following them for as far as she could see.

Soon they'd left London and were heading into the Kent countryside – further and further away from Woofer.

When Tiger Lily didn't come to the kitchen the next morning Woofer ran up the stairs to the king's apartments to see where she was. He scratched at the closed door and barked his deep bark but the door didn't open.

George found the puppy lying outside the king's door, waiting for Tiger Lily to come out and play, the rope toy beside him.

'She'll be back soon,' George told the little dog but Woofer just gave a big sigh and rested his head on his paws.

Teeth and Claws headed over to the turnspit wheel where they spent most of their days, but they weren't going in it today. Woofer was.

He was no longer a young puppy and George and Humphrey had decided it was time for him to learn how to be a turnspit dog. Woofer thought he'd rather play in the garden but he didn't have a choice as George lifted him up and put him inside the wheel.

Woofer wasn't sure what he was supposed to do and tried to jump out at first but soon realized he was shut in. The outside of the turnspit wheel had four spokes to it. The inside of the wheel had wooden struts built across it to stop the dogs from slipping. It was still hard for Woofer's paws to get a grip but it was easier than usual because the wheel had recently been given a good scrub.

Woofer thought he'd rather be on the ground and not in the wheel. He gave a whine.

'You're OK,' George reassured him. All of the kitchen dogs had to work, just as all of the kitchen staff had to. The life of the turnspit dogs was hard but at least they weren't on the streets and there was enough food for them.

'Put a bit of hot coal in with him, that'll speed him up,' said one of the kitchen boys.

George rolled his eyes. 'And when it burns his paws and he's limping, we'll be down a dog,' he said.

'And my meat won't be roasted then,' Humphrey said, flicking the boy's ear. 'Might as well put you in there with a bit of hot coal. Although it'd be a squeeze.'

Now the boy looked worried as he imagined what it would be like to be trapped in the wheel for hours.

'I'll empty the waste buckets,' he said, and hurried off.

George started to turn the wheel slowly to show Woofer what he needed to do.

'You've got to keep walking so the meat keeps turning round and round and doesn't get burnt and blackened,' he told him.

The wheel wasn't wide enough for a dog to lie down, even a small dog like Woofer, at least not comfortably, anyway. Woofer gave a whine and put out his paw to George. It broke George's heart but Woofer had to learn. He turned the wheel some more.

'That's it, Woofer!' he said as Woofer began to walk in the wheel. 'That's it – good dog.'

Woofer didn't like walking in the wheel very much, but he did like making George happy and so on he trotted.

'Good dog, Woofer,' Old Peg told him.

George gave him a sliver of meat as a reward.

'That's enough for today,' he told Woofer.

As soon as he opened the wheel Woofer jumped out of it and ran into the garden. He didn't want to go in there again.

'That's another reason why geese are better than dogs in the turnspit wheel,' Humphrey said.

'What do you mean?' George asked him.

'Geese don't run away or hide when they're supposed to be working,' Humphrey laughed.

Meanwhile, down in Kent, Tiger Lily watched the other royal dogs splashing about in the river with James Jack and the king. It had taken most of the last day of July to get to Tunbridge but once they were there the very first place James Jack had taken the dogs was a shallow part of the river so that they could cool down. After that they'd gone to the river every day and sometimes twice a day.

'Come on in, Tiger Lily,' the king called to her. But Tiger Lily wasn't ready to go in very far just yet and stayed on the bank cooling her paws. The next time she went to the river, though, she ventured in a little further. And the time after that, on a very hot day, she had her first doggy paddle.

By the time the visit to the spa town was over Tiger Lily loved going in the water. She showed no fear as she glided through it with hardly a splash. She'd even managed to catch a small trout, albeit by mistake, and the king had been so proud of her that he'd insisted it was cooked and presented to her for supper.

On the journey home to London, Tiger Lily sat either on her cushion, or the king's lap, a much happier puppy.

'The king and his Court are coming home at last,' Humphrey told the kitchen staff. George smiled. It had been nice to have the palace to themselves but it hadn't felt right without the normal hustle and bustle.

'Tiger Lily's finally coming home,' George whispered to Woofer.

Woofer tilted his head to one side as if he recognized Tiger Lily's name and then wagged his tail-stub. George was happy and that always made the little dog happy too.

Woofer stood next to George as the carriages came in through the palace gates. He didn't know quite what was going on, but everyone around him was excited and it was infectious.

Inside the royal coach Tiger Lily saw Woofer and stood up on her velvet cushion, which was placed next to the king, wagging her tail and yapping.

Woofer barked in reply, only his bark, like that of all Wicklow terriers, sounded as if it came from a much larger dog.

The next instant Tiger Lily jumped out of the carriage's open window and raced over to George and Woofer.

'Tiger Lily, come back!' the king shouted, and the carriage ground to a halt as did all the other carriages behind it.

George brought Tiger Lily back to the king, closely followed by Woofer.

'I see she hasn't forgotten you or her friend Woofer,' said the king. He opened the carriage door and Tiger Lily hopped in and Woofer hopped in after her.

'I'm sorry, sir,' George said, reaching in to haul Woofer out again but the king looked at the two dogs playing together and smiled.

'Get in too,' he told George.

George pointed at himself in surprise and then sat down opposite the king on the very edge of the crimson-silk seat that matched the crimson reins of the horses, and rode into the palace instead of walking as he'd always done before. He couldn't help thinking that Gran and Annie would never believe this when he told them!

Master Vogel saw George in the carriage and gritted his teeth. That kitchen boy was getting far above himself, riding with the king and with that mutt of a dog. If he had his way, there'd be no dogs in the palace kitchens, spreading fleas and diseases.

Chapter 7

Tiger Lily was delighted to be back home and she soon reacquainted herself with all her old favourite places, accompanied by her best friend Woofer. The kitchen was her first port of call, where she was given tasty treats and cuddles by Humphrey; then the king's secret doorway that lead out on to the banks of the river, and the Privy Garden where she and Woofer played and played.

One sunny day at the very beginning of September, as Old Peg was sitting huddled close to the fire, despite it being very hot in the kitchen, George and the dogs came back in from their morning walk. Half the time Old Peg seemed to be asleep, and no one liked to move her, so there she stayed by the fire. But that morning Old Peg's misty blue eyes suddenly flew open and she pointed at George.

'Go home!' she shouted at him. 'Go home right now!'

Something about the way she said it made him turn and run.

Woofer ran after him and George was too worried about his gran to take the dog back to the palace. Together they raced along Thames Street and up Fish Street Hill until they came to Black Raven Alley. The raggedy cat that always used to be on the roof wasn't there any more.

George was just about to open Gran's front door when he saw a plague doctor wearing a beaked mask stuffed full of flowers and herbs and a long overcoat. With him was a watchman with a cloth soaked in vinegar round the lower half of his face, carrying a stick. They headed down the cobblestoned alleyway towards George and his hand dropped from the latch, his heart beating very fast.

Cases of the plague were far less frequent now but people were still dying from it.

Woofer looked up at him and then back at the door.

George shook his head. He wanted to go inside but they couldn't. If Gran did have the plague then they might end up quarantined and not be let out again.

Woofer gave a whine. He could smell the delicious aroma of pottage gently stewing on the fire coming from inside the house.

'No, Woofer.'

George knocked on the door. 'Gran?' he called out. 'Gran, are you OK? Gran!'

But there was no reply.

'Plague?' the doctor asked George.

'I don't know, sir, I haven't been inside,' George told him.

The doctor lifted the latch and went in with the watchman while George and Woofer waited outside.

A few minutes later, the watchman came to the door and shook his head. 'You can see her if you want.'

Woofer raced past George as they went inside.

'Not the plague,' said the beak-masked doctor, squeezing George's shoulder. He pulled the mask that smelt of lavender, rosemary and garlic off his face. 'Just old age.'

Tears streamed down George's face as he looked at the pottage gently cooking over the fire. He had arrived just a bit too late. He forced himself to look at Gran's body. She looked very peaceful but George couldn't believe he'd never see her alive again. Woofer gazed up at him and whined. When George didn't react, the dog pushed his head under the boy's hand for a stroke and then rested his chin on George's leg, sharing his sadness.

There were arrangements to be made and Gran's things to be sorted out. George and Woofer spent the rest of that day and night at Black Raven Alley but they had to return to the palace the next morning.

The last thing George did before they left Gran's house was lift the iron pot of soup from its hook over the fire with a thick cloth. He couldn't bear to leave it behind and carried it through the streets as they walked back to the palace.

There'd been no rain for months and months and it was another hot day. People were heading out to Smithfield for the second week of Old Bartlemy's Fair.

Around him people laughed and joked and talked in the streets. George felt numb. He wanted to shake the passers-by and shout at them. Didn't they know what had happened? Didn't they understand his gran had just died and that nothing would ever be the same again?

Woofer whimpered.

When they arrived back at the palace kitchen an hour later Humphrey wasn't there and Master Vogel was now in charge of George's kitchen.

'Where've you been?' Master Vogel demanded to know.

George didn't reply, which made Master Vogel even angrier.

Old Peg wasn't in her usual spot but over by the door in a draught. George gave her some of Gran's soup and she slurped it noisily.

Woofer sat down and put his paw out and George poured him a bowl too.

'I asked where you've been!' Master Vogel shouted, so loudly that for a moment Woofer stopped lapping up his soup in surprise.

Everyone looked round at George and his face flushed hot. 'At my gran's,' he muttered.

But Master Vogel wasn't listening.

'There's no time for such laziness in my kitchen!' he yelled.

'Where's Humphrey?' George asked. Why was Master Vogel now in charge of the kitchen?

'If you'd been at work yesterday, as you should have been, you'd know,' Master Vogel said.

George tried to find out what had happened to Humphrey from one of the other kitchen staff but the boy he asked glanced over at Master Vogel's furious face and wouldn't say anything.

Woofer looked up at the sound of soft paw pads on the stone floor, so quiet that only a dog could hear.

Tiger Lily wagged her tail at the kitchen door and Woofer tilted his head as he looked over at George and then back at his friend. George wasn't paying him any attention, so he decided to join Tiger Lily as she trotted off to the Privy Garden. A butterfly flew in front of them and the two dogs gave chase as it danced among the flowers.

Inside the kitchen George heard a whine and when he looked over he saw that Scraps was in the turnspit wheel.

'What's she doing in there?' he cried.

Everyone in the kitchen knew that Scraps was too old to do much work any more.

'She's earning her keep,' Master Vogel told him. 'Unlike you, young man. Although she needed a hot coal or two thrown in with her every now and again to keep her moving. Nothing like a piece of hot coal in the wheel to keep a turnspit dog motivated.'

George felt sick as he ran over to the wheel and lifted Scraps out.

Master Vogel became even angrier when he saw what George was doing. 'I didn't say the wheeler could come out yet!'

'I'm so sorry,' George whispered into Scraps' fur. The dog was breathing heavily, a raspy, rattly breathing that George hadn't heard before. She didn't try to stand up but lay limp in his arms.

'Put her back in this instant!' Master Vogel shouted.

'Can't you see? She can't do any more,' George told him as a tear slipped down his face.

'Yes, she can!' Master Vogel bellowed. He was almost exploding with rage now because all the staff were looking at him. 'The wheeler's just being lazy – like most animals and people!'

George shook his head as he looked at Scraps' burnt paws. She'd had no chance of escaping the hot coals that Master Vogel had thrown in with her.

'Put her back in the wheel right now or you're fired!' Master Vogel roared so loudly George thought the whole palace could have heard him.

Scraps closed her eyes and after a big sigh she stopped breathing. She was gone.

Another tear slipped down George's face and he dashed it away.

'Get out!' Master Vogel yelled at George. 'Get out and don't come back!'

George stroked Scraps. He didn't want to leave her, even though she was no longer alive.

Master Vogel grabbed hold of George and shoved him out of the door. 'You're fired!'

Chapter 8

When Woofer and Tiger Lily grew tired of chasing butterflies they headed back to the king's apartment and helped themselves to the tasty treats that were always set out for the royal dogs on silver platters, as well as a long cool drink from the fresh water in the silver bowl.

The scent of mouse beneath the king's bed was too much for any dog to resist and certainly too much for Woofer. He dived under the heavy maroon velvet cover, embroidered with gold, that had fallen on the floor and disappeared while Tiger Lily watched from the top of the bed. She'd tried to catch the mouse under the mattress many times before, as had the rest of the king's dogs, but this creature had always managed to evade them.

Woofer was determined to succeed. He had the mouse cornered, only to miss it by a whisker as it escaped into a hole. As it did so he gave a whine of frustration but then froze as the king's bedroom door slammed shut. When he poked his head out from under the heavy bedcover on the floor, he found that Tiger Lily had been shut in too. Tiger Lily ran to the door and gave her high bark but it didn't open. Woofer tried barking his deeper, louder bark but that didn't work either. Tiger Lily stood on her back legs and scratched at the door but still no one came – not even when they both scratched and barked and barked. Finally they lay down by the door, rested their heads on their paws and waited for someone to let them out.

Eventually, the door was opened by the woman who came to empty the chamber pots, and Tiger Lily and Woofer raced out of the room and down the stairs to the kitchen.

But when they got there they found that George and the rest of the dogs were missing. No turnspits in the kitchen meant that the meat was burning on the spit.

'Grab him!' Master Vogel shouted, pointing at Woofer. He needed a dog in the wheel.

But Woofer didn't want to be grabbed and he certainly didn't want to go in the turnspit wheel. He ran out of the kitchen and back up the stairs with Tiger Lily close behind him.

'Don't just stand there – bring him back!' Master Vogel yelled, and the kitchen staff chased up the stairs after the two dogs.

As the kitchen apprentices charged after them, Tiger Lily led Woofer through the door that led from the king's apartment to the river and the two puppies raced along the muddy grey banks of the Thames.

The king was on his barge, returning from Greenwich, where he'd been inspecting the navy, when he saw Tiger Lily running along the riverbank.

'Tiger Lily, come back!' he shouted.

But Tiger Lily was in such a panic because of the kitchen staff chasing her that she didn't hear the king, and the two puppies kept on running. Woofer's nostrils were filled with a myriad smells along the rubbish-strewn riverbank: meat, fish and rotting vegetables. Anything that wasn't wanted was dumped in the river.

London Bridge was chaotic and noisy as always. It was crowded with buildings on top of it and boats passing through underneath.

Tiger Lily and Woofer were almost halfway across the bridge when they ran straight into the path of a black bear on a lead, being taken to Old Bartlemy's Fair by its owner. The animal growled at them and the puppies whimpered and ran back the other way.

The next instant a nut landed on Woofer's back and he yelped. A monkey on a pole pointed at him and made loud, angry chattering sounds. It threw a second nut, still in its hard shell. This one landed on Tiger Lily's head and although it hurt, she was more shocked by it than anything and the puppies ran on.

'Get out of the way!' shouted a man on stilts, also heading to the fair, as they almost tripped him up.

The puppies didn't stop running until they were gasping for breath and could run no more.

'Hello, my beauties,' said a red-headed girl sitting on the steps outside a theatre with a basket of oranges beside her. 'Hungry?' She laughed as she threw them a bit of the pork pie she'd been eating.

Tiger Lily and Woofer wagged their tails at the sound of a friendly voice and trotted over to her and gobbled up the greasy pork pie.

'Come on then, come and sit on the steps with Nellie,' the girl said, and she patted the space next to her. First Tiger Lily and then Woofer flopped down beside her.

'You are a very pretty puppy,' she told Tiger Lily, noting her long tail that meant she must belong to the nobility.

Woofer rolled over on to his back for a tummy rub. He was almost too wide for the step.

'And you're very handsome too,' Nell laughed as she rubbed his tummy.

'Nell, come back in and bring those oranges with you!' a voice shouted from the theatre doorway.

'But –'

'Now!'

Nell gave the dogs a last look and hurried back inside.

A few moments later, hundreds of sheep came down the street, being driven towards the two puppies on the steps by three men, two women and a boy, plus four sheepdogs.

The sheepdogs were too busy making sure the sheep stayed together and didn't stray into other streets to pay any attention to Woofer or Tiger Lily. But one of the sheep ran up the steps towards them.

Tiger Lily and Woofer quickly backed away as more sheep followed the first one. The sheepdogs climbed the steps to round up the strays, and before they knew it Tiger Lily and Woofer were being swept along the narrow streets in the middle of a giant flock of sheep.

'Get out of the way!' people were shouting as they tried to get past but the flock stopped for no one. And the sheepdogs kept their charges moving by nipping at their heels. Tiger Lily didn't like being squashed by the sheep on either side. They were much bigger and heavier than she was and she yelped when one of them stepped on her paw.

Finally the sheep stopped at the livestock market and Woofer and Tiger Lily were able to break free as the sheepdogs helped to sort the animals into pens.

All around them were other creatures waiting to be sold. Cows to the right of them and pigs to the left. A baby goat managed to escape by hopping on top of another goat in its pen and there was chaos for a few moments until it was caught.

Tiger Lily stepped backwards in surprise and found herself in a pile of manure. A cow lowered its head and mooed at her and Tiger Lily let out a squeak of terror, backing even further into the manure. The stink was overpowering to a dog's sensitive nose and even more so to Tiger Lily. The only time she'd ever got muddy was when she played along the riverbank with Woofer – and that had always been swiftly followed by a bath. She held up one paw and then the other but there was nothing that could be done and no one to clean her.

Tiger Lily whimpered.

Woofer only narrowly avoided being trodden on by a sow.

'Here, what're these dogs doing here?' someone yelled.

One of the farmers noted Tiger Lily's long tail. He was well aware that undocked dogs belonged to the nobility and there was often a reward for their return.

'Anyone see who it's with?' he asked another farmer.

'Grab hold of it, Michael.'

But as the farmer's boy tried to grab Tiger Lily the baby goat managed to escape again and Woofer and Tiger Lily ran off as the farmers at the livestock market tried to catch it.

*

When George left the kitchen, Teeth and Claws ran after him.

'Go back!' George said, pointing to the door they'd come out of, but Teeth and Claws didn't go back, and when George carried on walking out of the palace gates they looked at each other and then trotted along behind him.

George knew he couldn't keep the dogs and would have to take them back but he didn't want to. Master Vogel was a bully and he didn't want Teeth and Claws to have to work for him. But he didn't have a choice.

'Come on,' George coaxed, as he turned round and slowly headed back, followed by Teeth and Claws.

As George returned through the gates and into the palace grounds with the two dogs, he ran into James Jack who was looking very anxious.

'Tiger Lily's missing and so is Woofer,' he said and explained that they had been seen running along the riverbank. 'The king's issued a proclamation for her return.'

George was so worried he could barely listen to it. '*For the dog was not born nor bred in England, and would never forsake her master. A most handsome reward will be paid to whoever finds her and returns her safely to His Majesty.*'

All he knew was that the puppies had run away. It wasn't safe for Woofer and Tiger Lily to be out on the streets alone. Anything could happen to them.

George's stomach churned with fear. He had to find them!

James Jack headed off to gather more people to help with the search as George ran to the riverbank with Teeth and Claws right behind him.

Tiger Lily wasn't used to being pushed this way and that in the crowded streets. Or having to avoid feet and carts and animals that got in her way. Her life at the palace was nothing like life on the London streets.

'Look out below!' a voice shouted and a bucket of rank, stinking water came pouring out of an upstairs window and landed directly on top of Tiger Lily, soaking her through.

Tiger Lily yelped as it hit her and then whimpered as the foul-smelling liquid sank into her fur. Her head drooped. She didn't know where she was or how to get home. Everything felt strange. She was quite, quite lost as she followed Woofer down the cobblestoned streets. Her paws were sore and her coat was smelly. All she wanted was a long drink of cool water and something tasty to eat.

Woofer sniffed the air. It was full of fishy smells that he remembered clearly. Now he knew where they should go. He gave a woof and Tiger Lily ran after him as he raced up Fish Street Hill to Black Raven Alley. He stopped outside George's gran's house and woofed again.

The raggedy cat was back and it stared down at Tiger Lily from its spot on the sloping roof, its eyes almost hypnotizing. Tiger Lily had never met a cat close up before. She tilted her head to one side and wagged her tail tentatively in greeting.

Woofer gave another friendly bark and the cat crept down and sniffed at them before hopping back on to the roof.

When Gran's front door didn't open Woofer scratched at it with his paw and barked once again.

The door still didn't open but the one next to it did.

'Go on, be off with you!' a voice shouted at Woofer but then stopped when the speaker saw Tiger Lily – a smelly wet dog covered in manure, with a long undocked tail.

She had to be a noble dog because of her tail, even if she wasn't actually one of the royal dogs. Gran's neighbour Jed thought there might be a good reward for the return of the bedraggled-looking spaniel standing just out of reach and looking sorry for itself.

'Here, missy, here,' Jed said in a wheedling sort of voice.

Tiger Lily was tired of running through the streets after Woofer. The streets didn't smell nice and now she didn't smell nice either because of the slop that had landed on top of her. She took a step towards the man in the doorway.

'That's it,' Jed said, bending down and stretching out a hand towards her, ready to grab the little dog as soon as she came close enough. He wondered how big a reward he would get for finding a noble dog.

Tiger Lily took another step forward and Jed's hand was just about to close round the scruff of her neck when the raggedy cat gave a loud warning yowl and the next instant the two puppies ran off together.

'No! Wait! Stop – come back!' Jed shouted and went running after them, which only made the dogs run faster.

Down one alleyway, up another, through a gap in a wall and out on to the street. Jed soon lost sight of the dogs and returned home angry that he had missed out on some much-needed cash.

The foul-smelling water that had soaked her through had dried into Tiger Lily's coat by the time Woofer smelt another aroma that he remembered – delicious, crunchy, ginger-flavoured dog biscuits!

Woofer barked and trotted on ahead while a less-than-happy Tiger Lily followed, her long peacock-feather tail drooping sadly.

Chapter 9

Saturday night and early Sunday morning

George started his search where Tiger Lily and Woofer had last been seen but once he came to London Bridge he had no idea which way they'd gone. Could Woofer have remembered the way to Gran's house from the palace? She'd always been kind to the little dog when she'd been alive. Maybe, just maybe, he'd taken Tiger Lily there for safety.

It was worth a try.

'Come on,' he said to Teeth and Claws, and they ran after him as he raced down the streets towards Gran's house.

George swallowed hard as he went up Fish Street Hill followed by the dogs. Claws gulped down a tasty fishtail he found lying on the ground. Teeth swallowed a discarded fish head.

'Oysters, fresh oysters.'

'Trout to buy, trout to buy . . .'

Teeth and Claws looked over at the fish sellers as they called out their wares but George barely heard their cries. All he could think about was finding Woofer and Tiger Lily.

'This way,' he said to the dogs as he turned into Black Raven Alley.

Teeth and Claws looked up at the raggedy cat on the roof and her tail twitched as she stared back at them.

George was now in front of Gran's door and he steeled himself to open it and go back inside.

But before he could lift the latch her neighbour's door opened.

'Come to see what the old lady left?' Jed asked him.

George had met Jed a couple of times before but he'd never been very keen on the man.

Jed looked at Teeth and Claws but they didn't go up to him for a stroke and kept close to George.

'Have you seen two dogs in the alley?' George asked. 'One is a terrier and the other a spaniel.' He didn't trust Gran's neighbour enough to tell him that Tiger Lily was the king's dog.

'What if I have?' Jed said.

'Have you?' George asked, his heart lifting.

'Depends. What'd there be in it for me?'

Now George was stumped. He didn't have anything to give the man. All he had in his pocket was Woofer and Tiger Lily's rope toy.

'Nothing.'

'Well then I've seen *nothing.*'

But George knew that he had seen something by the way he spoke. He thought quickly as Jed started to close the door.

'You'd have the palace's gratitude.'

Jed stopped closing the door. 'How much gratitude?'

George didn't know and he couldn't keep on lying so he said, 'The king would be very grateful.'

'Well then – two dogs were here. One of them a spaniel, the other a lot like those two you have there. Short-legged and long-bodied. You make sure you tell the king I helped you and would like to see some gratitude in my hand.'

'Where are they now?' George asked.

'Ran off,' Jed told him, and he pointed in the direction Tiger Lily and Woofer had gone, back towards London Bridge where George had just come from.

'Thank you,' George said as he hurried out of the alley and back along Fish Street Hill and down Thames Street with Teeth and Claws at his heels. It was getting very late and growing dark.

Outside the theatre he asked a girl selling oranges if she'd seen two dogs, one dock-tailed and one undocked.

'I think I did see them,' she said, describing Woofer and Tiger Lily almost exactly. 'It was a few hours ago now, though.'

'And was the spaniel well?'

'Oh, yes. Very well, judging by how she gobbled down the pork pie I threw to her and her friend.'

George smiled. Woofer and Tiger Lily both had very good appetites. And that gave him an idea of where they might have gone.

'The king will be glad to hear of your kindness,' he said to the girl as he hurried off towards Pudding Lane. 'What's your name?'

'Nell,' she said. 'My name's Nell Gwynne.'

*

Woofer gave a bark and a wag of his tail-stub as an exhausted Tiger Lily flopped down beside him on the cobblestones. The little dog was very pleased with himself. He'd found the place where he'd first tried the delicious biscuits. It had taken them a bit longer than it should have done because he'd been distracted by the smell of a freshly baked sweet and savoury mince pie but they had finally made it. Now all he needed to do was get someone to open the door. Woofer woofed.

Upstairs in her room above the bakery, Annie woke up. She'd been dreaming that she was making cakes for a royal banquet. Hundreds and hundreds of cakes, but however fast she worked, still more were needed. Then something had woken her and she wasn't quite sure what it was. In the darkness she listened to the sounds of the night. A strong easterly wind rattled the shop sign on its rusty hinges and whistled through the chimney stacks but that wasn't what had woken her.

Woofer gave another woof.

To Annie the bark sounded like it was coming from a large dog, although it didn't seem angry or aggressive, just very insistent. As if it needed something and couldn't wait. As if it was right outside the bakery door downstairs.

Annie rubbed at her eyes as she crept over to the window to look out. On the cobblestones below she was amazed to find that there wasn't the giant, ferocious dog she'd expected to see, but a small cream-coated, short-legged, long-bodied, funny-faced terrier and a delicate-looking spaniel.

The terrier's bark became even louder and more frequent when he saw her at the window.

'Woofer!' Annie cried, and she ran down the stairs and into the bakery. As she hurried to the door she heard the spaniel barking too, only that bark was much higher-pitched. Then both dogs started scratching at the door.

'All right, all right, hang on a second,' Annie said as she pulled back the heavy bolts.

Woofer gave another of his deep woofs to hurry her along and Annie quickly opened the door.

'Well, hello there, Woofer,' she said. 'Brought a friend with you, I see.'

But why wasn't George with them? She hoped nothing bad had happened to him.

Woofer wagged his tail-stub. Tiger Lily was still feeling miserable from the unexpected smelly-water shower, so she didn't come forward as she would normally, with a wag of her beautiful tail, but held back a little instead.

'Shy?' Annie asked, kneeling down and holding out a hand to the spaniel, and at last Tiger Lily padded towards her. 'That's it,' Annie said as she led them inside. She reached into a sack and gave Tiger Lily a piece of broken biscuit. Tiger Lily gently took it from her and then looked up for more.

Woofer gave a bark to remind Annie not to forget him.

'Shhh,' Annie said as she gave him some biscuit too. The dogs were both very hungry. 'That's enough for now,' she told them when they'd had five each.

Annie realized she'd have to stay down here with the dogs because Mr Farriner didn't like them in the house. Mrs Farriner had died of the plague almost a year ago to the day and Mr Farriner still thought an infected dog might have been the cause of it. No one knew for sure but he wasn't taking any chances.

At least it was a bit cooler downstairs. Plus she'd hear George straight away if he came looking for the dogs. It was so strange that he wasn't with them, but finding him would have to wait until morning now. Annie yawned and laid out an empty flour sack for the dogs to lie on and another for herself.

Tiger Lily sniffed at the sacking. She was used to being fed on the finest food and sleeping on a soft cushion at the palace, but the biscuits had been delicious and sacking made a comfortable-enough bed, especially with Woofer there, and she soon fell fast asleep.

They hadn't been asleep for long when Woofer smelt smoke and opened his eyes. Tiger Lily was awake too and she sat up.

Woofer woke Annie with a slobbery lick on her face.

'Yeuwk!' Annie said, rubbing at her cheek. 'What did you do that for?'

Tiger Lily gave a frightened yap.

But Annie had seen the fire and was already scrambling to her feet. The pile of wood beside the oven, placed there ready for the next morning, was ablaze.

'Teagh!' Annie screamed as she grabbed the almost-empty pail of water and threw it at the flames. 'Teagh!'

There wasn't enough water in the bucket to make any difference. The wood was so dry that it caught like a match.

'Teagh!' Annie screamed again and at last she heard movement upstairs. 'Fire!'

Teagh ran down the stairs but was prevented from coming into the bakery by the fire. The room was quickly filling with black smoke.

'Get out!' he shouted as he dashed back upstairs to warn his employer.

Annie grabbed the sack of dog biscuits and ran out of the bakery door on to the street, followed by Woofer and Tiger Lily.

Seconds later the bakery was an inferno. If the dogs hadn't been there she didn't know if any of them would have woken up in time. She clutched the biscuits to her as she looked up at the first-floor window.

In the street, above the sound of the flames, Annie could hear Teagh shouting and pounding at the sleeping Farriners' doors. She coughed because the smoke from the building was growing thicker by the second.

Tiger Lily trembled as she and Woofer stayed close to Annie. The smoke made the spaniel's large brown eyes stream. The crackling sound sent waves of fear through her. All she wanted to do was run far, far away from this terrible place but she stayed because Woofer didn't run.

A few moments later Mr Farriner climbed out of a window at the top of the house and on to the roof. Annie put her hand to her mouth as she watched him rest a foot on the gutter and reach back for Hannah. Teagh followed her.

Mr Farriner, Hannah and Teagh crawled along the roof to the garret window of the neighbour's house. Mr Farriner banged on the leaded glass but no one came. Annie ran to the front door of the house they were trying to get into and started pounding on it.

'Fire!' she cried. 'Fire!'

The door and garret window opened at the same time and Mr Farriner, Hannah and Teagh were able to climb inside.

Hannah was crying now that they were safe – great noisy sobs interspersed with coughing – and the neighbours were getting ready to leave their house, taking whatever they could with them.

'How did it start?' Hannah croaked. 'How could it have happened? Our home. Everything gone. You weren't doing more of your silly cooking experiments, were you, Annie?'

Annie shook her head as tears streamed down her hot sooty face. She didn't know why the fire had started – Mr Farriner was always so particular about checking it was extinguished before he went to bed.

They went outside and gazed as the roof that they'd been able to escape along blazed.

Tiger Lily watched and whimpered. A man with a leather bucket of water almost tripped over her small body. 'Get out of it, you stupid dog!' he yelled at her.

Tiger Lily had never been shouted at before today and this was the final straw. She turned and ran and ran and ran. Woofer saw her racing off towards Fish Street Hill and charged after his friend but Tiger Lily had longer legs and was much quicker than him.

She wanted to be back home with people she knew who were kind to her, where there was a soft bed and tasty food. But she didn't know the way back to the palace and in her panic she ran further and further away from it.

They hadn't gone far up Fish Street Hill when George smelt smoke and saw flames.

'No!' he gasped, when they turned into Pudding Lane. The bakery was ablaze. Had Woofer and Tiger Lily come here? Were the dogs still inside?

He ran towards the fire, and Teeth and Claws ran after him. They were hampered by the furniture, beds, boxes, trading stock and belongings from other houses along the lane that had been put there to save them if the fire spread.

All around were cries of 'Fire! Fire!' as people woke up their sleeping neighbours. The church bells of Fish Street Hill were ringing in reverse to warn everyone. A thunder of drums called people to come and help fight the blaze.

'Annie!' George yelled to the people rushing about and trying to put out the flames. 'Have you seen a girl called Annie? She works in there!'

But no one had seen her and they didn't have time for questions as they passed along buckets and bowls and chamber pots filled with water and mud and earth and anything else that might help dampen the flames.

'Did everyone get out safely?' George asked desperately.

'Not sure.'

'Don't know,' passers-by told him.

'What about Annie? Did you see Annie?' George asked the elderly candlemaker, who lived a few doors along.

'She wasn't with the baker and his daughter and manservant when they climbed out of that window,' the candlemaker told him as he pointed up at a window that was now in flames.

George gave a hacking cough. It was getting harder to breathe.

'The baker's gone to get the fire squirts,' someone said.

George, Teeth and Claws ran to Butchers' Hill where the brass fire squirts were stored.

'Did you see two dogs?' he asked the men coming back with them.

'Why are you talking about dogs at a time like this?' they shouted.

'Baker doesn't have a dog,' one man told him as George helped to carry the heavy fire-fighting equipment back down the hill. Each fire squirt took three people to work it – two to hold the handles and one to push the plunger.

'One of them's a spaniel and the other a Wicklow terrier,' George shouted to a woman collecting water from a thin stream made by a burst water pipe. It was hard to make himself heard above the chaos and uproar all around him.

'No!' she shouted back as someone cried for help.

George ran to help with the fire squirt as one of the men holding the handles stumbled on the now hot and slippery cobbles.

'I saw a dog. Almost tripped over the silly thing. A spaniel. Sent it on its way,' the man pressing the plunger told him.

'Had another one, funny-looking short-legged thing, running after it,' said the man who'd stumbled, as he took back his place from George.

George breathed a huge sigh of relief. Someone had seen them and not long ago. But where were they? Was Annie with them? And was she OK?

The house next to the baker's was now engulfed in flames and the one after that was smouldering. It was difficult to breathe because of all the smoke.

'Which way did they go?' George asked.

The man pointed him in the direction he'd seen the dogs heading, so George turned and ran, with Teeth and Claws right behind him.

Chapter 10

Sunday 2 September 1666

At dawn Woofer found Tiger Lily curled up on the steps leading to a grand house in Gracechurch Street at the top of Fish Street Hill. She was panting, trembling with fear and utterly miserable. Her coat not only smelt of slops now but of smoke too.

Woofer went to his friend and lay down beside her. Tiger Lily pressed herself close to him and gradually her trembling ceased and the two dogs fell asleep, only to be woken by three men almost trampling them as they ran up the steps and thumped on the front door.

'Sir Thomas! Sir Thomas! We have an emergency!' they told the man in his nightclothes who opened the door.

'What sort of an emergency?' Sir Thomas asked as he rubbed his sleepy eyes.

'The fire, sir . . .'

Sir Thomas frowned. 'I've already been to see the fire during the night and it's nothing to worry about. It'll soon burn itself out. Now let me get back to bed.'

'No, Mr Bloodworth, sir, I mean, Your Worshipfulness,' one of the men said, taking off his cap and wringing it in his hands. 'The fire's spread.'

'It's not going to burn itself out now,' said the second man.

'We have to do something, Lord Mayor . . .' insisted the third man. 'It's burning everything before it.'

‘We could pull down houses in the fire’s path,’ suggested the first man.

‘Yes – and who’ll pay for them to be rebuilt!’ the lord mayor replied as he emerged from the house, pulling the door closed behind him. The law said that any man destroying another man’s home had to pay for it to be rebuilt. He couldn’t afford that.

‘Get out of the way, dogs!’ the lord mayor ordered as he passed them.

Tiger Lily cowered from him and he didn’t notice her long tail.

As the men and Sir Thomas strode off down the street she and Woofer trotted after them as the cobblestones grew hotter beneath their paws.

Fish Street Hill was ablaze and the flames were now heading towards London Bridge. Showers of sparks leapt across to Thames Street

Suddenly there was a massive explosion on the waterfront as one of the warehouses that was filled with pitch and oil exploded. People looked on, horrified.

'It's too late!' they cried.

'We're all doomed!'

'It's God's wrath!'

The explosion knocked Tiger Lily and Woofer to the ground as it shuddered through them with a bang so loud it left their ears ringing. They scrambled up and raced away from the blast but the fire followed them as two long arms of flames spread down Thames Street.

Tiger Lily ran and ran as Woofer panted his way after her, his tongue lolling out and his throat raw. The cobblestones grew cooler beneath their sore paws the further away from the fire they got and finally the smoke cleared a little, although the scent of it was everywhere.

Ahead of them was a horse trough and they both stood on their hind legs to have a long drink. Tiger Lily's tail wagged as her thirst was quenched.

A seven-year-old boy was looking out of an upstairs window in the house opposite and saw the dogs drinking.

'It's her,' he said to his mother, pointing at Tiger Lily and Woofer.

His mother didn't have time to ask him what he was talking about. She was stuffing as many of their belongings as she could into sacks for them to carry. The flames were soaring up into the sky nearby and they had to get as far away from the fire as they could. The smell of smoke was everywhere and the sun shone like blood.

'The dog in the proclamation. The king's missing dog,' the boy said.

Finally his mum looked over at the bedraggled spaniel and the terrier that was with her.

'Maybe,' she said doubtfully.

'It is. I know it is,' her son insisted. 'Look at her tail.'

Now that Woofer's thirst was quenched his hunger returned and when a rat scuttled past, his heart started thumping fast with excitement. He'd seen Teeth and Claws catch rats in the palace kitchen but he'd never actually caught one himself. He'd never been hungry enough to do so before. But now he was.

Tiger Lily's pink tongue came out and she licked her lips. She was very hungry too.

When Woofer saw a second rat, he raced after it but this one was too quick for him and it scuttled into the small muddy gap beneath the water trough.

Tiger Lily crouched down and peered into the dark space. She could see the rat's black eyes staring back at her.

Woofer lay down on the other side of the trough. Now all they had to do was wait. Woofer's tummy rumbled.

'Did it say there'd be a reward?' the boy's mother asked him.

'Bound to be,' said the boy. 'The king's got lots of money.'

His mother handed him one of the sacks she'd been packing their belongings into. They could buy new things with the reward money.

She smiled for the first time that day as they made their way down the stairs and over to the horse trough.

The rat beneath the trough seemed in no hurry to come out and get eaten.

Woofer put his head close to the ground and growled at it to get a move on. Tiger Lily lay on her side and stretched a paw into the narrow space beneath the trough.

Both of them were far too busy to pay any attention to the boy and his mother who were creeping towards them.

Suddenly something black and burnt landed on top of Woofer and he spun round in surprise and grabbed it in his teeth. The rat took the opportunity to race past him into a hole in the wall as Tiger Lily gave a yap of annoyance and Woofer realized he'd got food in his mouth – a roasted pigeon that had fallen out of the sky.

Woofer wagged his tail-stub as he trotted back to Tiger Lily with his prize, just as the boy and his mother reached the little spaniel.

'Quick! Catch her,' the boy's mother said, and the boy brought down the sack on top of Tiger Lily's head as she gave a surprised yelp. Woofer barked and dropped the pigeon.

'That's it,' the boy's mother said as Tiger Lily twisted and turned and tried desperately, but unsuccessfully, to scratch her way out of the sack.

'Get out of it, dog!' the boy said, pushing Woofer away with his foot when the terrier tried to help his friend.

'Put her on the handcart. We'll take her to the palace in that. It'll be easier than struggling through the streets with her,' said the boy's mother.

Woofer tried to stop them from taking his friend away by running in front of the three-wheeled cart but the boy just shoved it into him. Woofer yelped as it went over his paw.

The boy and his mother pushed the handcart down the street with the royal spaniel in a sack on top of their belongings and a small terrier with a sore paw running after them.

Inside the sack Tiger Lily tried to bite her way out, but the sacking was heavy and it was hard to get a grip on it with her teeth.

She didn't know where they were going but she could hear Woofer barking every now and again and knew that he was close behind.

'He'll soon give up and stop following us,' the boy's mother said. But Woofer didn't stop. He followed them through the crowds of people pushing and shoving their way down the streets as they tried to escape from the fire.

'Get out of the way, dog!'

Luckily Woofer could hear Tiger Lily whining and barking every now and again, although he couldn't always see her.

'What've you got in there?' a man asked the boy's mother, nodding at the wriggling bundle that was Tiger Lily.

'Nothing.'

'I can see it's something.'

The woman wasn't going to say any more but her son had been thinking about what he was going to spend the money on.

'It's the king's dog. We're going to return it to the palace and get a big reward.'

'I see,' the man said. 'That's very interesting indeed.' And the next moment he'd grabbed the sack that had Tiger Lily in it and was running off, barging his way through the crowds.

'Stop! Come back!' the boy and his mother cried.

The boy ran after the man while his mother stayed with their cart. They didn't want to lose that as well as the royal dog.

Woofer pushed his way past boots and shoes to catch up with the cart but he could sense something was wrong. Tiger Lily wasn't there and he didn't know where she'd gone.

'I lost them,' the boy said as he returned to his mother, shaking his head.

Woofer looked up at them and barked.

'We could take this one back to the king instead.'

'Don't be silly. He wouldn't want a dock-tailed dog, would he?'

Woofer tried to get a scent of Tiger Lily amid the thousands of people and animals that were moving down the streets. But there were too many smells. He tried for hours and hours with no luck.

It was the middle of the night by now but the sky was still bright because of the fire.

Woofer threw back his head and howled in despair.

The sounds of the fire and the throng all around him almost drowned out the noise but two turnspit dogs heard it. Teeth and Claws looked at each other and immediately made off in the direction of the howling.

George coughed as he followed them. There was no way to avoid the smoke that filled the air. It stung his eyes until they felt red-raw.

He'd lost Gran and Scraps and probably his friend Annie. He didn't know if Tiger Lily and Woofer were still alive or if they'd been caught by the fire. When he'd turned back into Black Raven Alley and seen his gran's house burnt to a cinder, like all the other houses in the street, the full force of it had swept over him and he'd sunk to his knees and wept.

Teeth and Claws had done their best to comfort him by whining and pushing their heads under his hand to be stroked.

George was glad Gran wasn't there to see her home destroyed.

'You'd have liked her and you'd have liked her soup,' he'd told Teeth and Claws, and his voice cracked as the dogs looked at him with their heads tilted to one side as if they were really listening. 'And she'd have loved you.'

No one was going to taste Gran's ever-bubbling pottage again.

The heat and acrid smoke meant his eyes still streamed long after he'd stopped weeping. There was no point in crying any longer. He knew he had to carry on to find Tiger Lily and Woofer, if they were still alive. No, he wouldn't even consider that. They had to be alive.

He followed Teeth and Claws as they headed down one street and up another.

Thames Street was in flames and impossible to get through so they had to double back to get round it. London Bridge was on fire too and the watermill beneath it was alight. With a great crash it tore free and floated off down the river, narrowly missing one of the hundreds of small boats piled high with people and their belongings trying to escape the fire's path.

Teeth and Claws stopped. They were at the spot where Woofer had howled up at the moon but the terrier had gone.

Chapter 11

Monday 3 September 1666

Tiger Lily was bumped and bruised inside the sack as her captor ran down one alleyway and up another, breathing heavily.

He checked behind him once again before finally slowing to a walk.

'You're going to make me very rich, you are!' he said.

Tiger Lily was frantically wriggling inside the sack, desperate to escape, but the man just laughed and tightened his hold on it.

He turned into Poultry Lane, known for all the ducks, chickens and geese that were bought and sold there, and lifted the latch of a dark, noisy house.

Tiger Lily smelt the scent of chickens and heard them all squawking as the man carried her inside.

'Stop that racket!' he growled at the birds but it only made them squawk louder.

The man lifted the top of an empty wooden chicken cage, undid the sack and tipped Tiger Lily in. He was so quick that Tiger Lily didn't have time to react before she fell into the cage with a thump.

There was barely enough room for Tiger Lily to move inside the cage and she barked and growled at the man, then started to bite at the bars with her teeth.

'None of that now,' the man said, and he threw some of the chickens' drinking water at her.

The shock of it made her stop biting the bars, and it also reminded the man that he was very thirsty after running around the city. But he didn't want water – he wanted ale and went out to buy some.

Tiger Lily was left in the room with about thirty chickens. It was dingy, dark and smelly. Now the man had gone the chickens didn't squawk any more but clucked as they stared at the new arrival with their sharp eyes.

Tiger Lily looked closely at the cage. The bars were made of wood and she had chewed through twigs before. She started gnawing at the bars. It wasn't easy because the cage was so small and there wasn't much room for manoeuvre. Eventually she managed to bite through one bar but she still wasn't free.

The chickens barely made a sound as they watched her.

As she bit through a second bar the chickens started squawking again and this time their squawks were much more desperate.

Tiger Lily sniffed the air. She could smell the fire. It was getting closer, much closer. She could hear the crackle of flames as the houses further along Poultry Lane caught light.

There wasn't enough time to bite through all the bars. Tiger Lily looked up at the top of the cage into which she'd been dropped. She pushed against the lid with her head and it moved. She pushed again and it moved some more. One final push and the lid flipped open and Tiger Lily scrambled out and was free.

The chickens had seen what she'd done to get out of the cage and they did the same and soon all the chickens, as well as Tiger Lily, were free of their cages and milling around the room.

The fire was now very, very close, so close that the walls started to blacken. Desperately Tiger Lily pushed at the door with her nose. It had worked at the palace if a door wasn't quite closed but this one was.

The smoke was getting thicker and the room was very hot. Tiger Lily barked and scratched at the door, gasping for air.

Suddenly it swung open.

'Can't lose my reward,' the man said. His jaw dropped when he saw all the freed chickens, and they squawked and pecked and flapped around him.

'What's going on?' he shouted as Tiger Lily ran past him into the burning street and the chickens ran out after her. She raced towards the river, knowing that she had to get back to the palace. The chickens soon fell behind and she was running alone, running for her life, towards the boats, furniture and people that filled the River Thames.

The wind blew great flakes of flame up into the sky and one of them landed on Woofer, singeing his fur and making him cry out in pain.

He'd been looking for Tiger Lily for such a long time. His paws were sore, he'd had no sleep and barely anything to eat.

But Woofer wouldn't give up and he searched on and on for his friend, returning to the riverside every now and again to get away from the flames.

At first when he saw the spaniel far in the distance along the riverbank he couldn't quite believe that he'd actually found her. As he got closer there was no doubt and he gave a deep bark of pure delight that was caught by the wind and spun in the other direction. He raced towards her as fast as his short legs would go.

But Tiger Lily hadn't heard Woofer's bark and she was looking towards the water not the riverbank. Before he could reach her she jumped into the river and swam towards the nearest boat, despite the terrible smell that was coming from it.

A hand grabbed her by the scruff of the neck and pulled her on board.

Now the smell was even worse and Tiger Lily gagged and brought up the water she'd swallowed. But at least she was away from the fire and the man who'd trapped her.

'Don't get many stowaways on dungboats,' the man said as Tiger Lily shook herself dry, and the boat carried on down the river with the manure that was used on the fields to help the crops grow. Fire or not, there was always manure to be spread.

On the riverbank Woofer barked and barked as his friend sailed further and further away.

Tiger Lily hadn't heard him and now she and the smelly boat were almost gone. Woofer whined and looked at the deep dark river full of boats, big and small, all of them overflowing with people, and then back at the vessel in the distance on which Tiger Lily was drifting away.

He hopped from one paw to the other, and stretched out a paw to the water but then put it back on the ground. He wanted to follow Tiger Lily but he didn't want to go in the river. He'd never been out of his depth, not even in the shallow lake at St James's Park, and this water was much deeper and dirtier than that.

On the riverbank it was getting hotter and the wind changed direction so that the air was now filled with thick smoke. Woofer gave an involuntary whimper. His friend needed him. Woofer's heart was racing but he closed his eyes and jumped in. The shock of the water made him open his mouth and swallow a great gulp of it.

He'd never swum before and he panicked, sinking and then bobbing back to the surface, coughing and spluttering and kicking his legs like mad.

The river was full of floating debris. Woofer couldn't see Tiger Lily's boat because his eyes were so full of water. Nor did he see the boat oar crashing down until it was too late.

'Look out!'

Woofer felt a searing pain in the back of his head just before he sank below the surface of the water.

'Have you seen two dogs?' George asked everybody rushing past him. But no one had time to stop. No one had time to care about the fate of an animal. 'One of them belongs to the king,' George called out. 'There's a reward.' But even that wasn't enough to halt the desperate people.

The fire was growing stronger and spreading further with every second that passed.

'George! George!' a voice cried and when he looked round he saw Annie running towards him.

'You survived!' George shouted as he ran towards her, and the two of them threw their arms round each other and hugged. Then Annie threw her arms round Teeth and Claws too and they wagged their tails and sniffed at the biscuits in the small sack she was holding.

'I'm so glad to see you.'

'I thought you were . . . were . . .' George said, and Annie knew what he was trying to say.

'Well, I'm not,' she said as she looked around. 'Where're Woofer and his friend?'

George shook his head. 'I don't know. I've been searching for them everywhere.'

'They were at the bakery,' Annie said, and she told him how the two puppies had alerted her to the fire. 'Without them I wouldn't be alive,' she added gravely.

George squeezed her hand. 'We have to find them,' he said.

Annie nodded and sniffed back her tears.

'But they could be anywhere.'

It seemed hopeless. Then Annie had an idea. 'Maybe your dogs could help.'

'Teeth and Claws? How?'

'My dad used to give the dogs the scent of a rabbit when they went out hunting and they'd go and look for it.'

George was doubtful that Teeth and Claws could do that.

'A dog's sense of smell is much better than a person's,' Annie said.

But George still shook his head. Teeth and Claws would not only have to catch the scent of Tiger Lily and Woofer in the air, they'd have to do so when the air all around them was full of smoke.

'It's worth a try,' Annie insisted. 'Do you have anything with the scent of Tiger Lily or Woofer on it?'

George was about to say no, but then he started grinning because he remembered that he did have something with the scent of both dogs on it. Something that both dogs loved to play with.

He pulled the rope toy from his pocket as Annie took two hard biscuits from her sack and gave one to each of the dogs.

'Find,' George commanded as he got the dogs to sniff at the rope toy. 'Find!' he repeated, and pointed away from him.

'Find,' said Annie and she pointed away too.

'They won't understand what to do,' George said. 'They've never done search-and-rescue work before.'

But as they watched, Teeth took another sniff of the rope toy and so did Claws. The two dogs looked at each other and then they ran off.

'Quick!' said Annie and she and George raced after them.

The smoke burnt George's throat and he coughed and coughed, trying to catch his breath as they ran.

'Here, put this round your face,' Annie said, and she gave him her apron that she'd soaked in water. 'It'll help.'

The man steering the dungboat stroked Tiger Lily with one hand as they sailed on down the river. Tiger Lily very much liked being stroked and soon even the smell of dung didn't seem so bad as they headed on out into the countryside.

They pulled up at a jetty and a farmer and his men arrived to collect the dung to spread on the fields. Even out here it was smoky and the flames were still visible in the distance. But dung had to be collected, fire or no fire.

'That's a fine-looking dog you have there, Peter,' the farmer said to the dung-boat worker.

'Yes, she is, and a good swimmer too. Swam right over to the boat. Nice to have a bit of company for a change. I think I'm going to keep her and we can sail up and down the

Thames together. Dora would be a good name for her, don't you think?'

But the farmer shook his head.

'You can't keep her,' he said. 'Not unless you want to be in a whole heap of trouble if you get caught.'

'Why not?' Peter wanted to know.

'Look at her tail. She's a nobleman's dog. Common folks like us have to have our dogs' tails docked.'

Peter looked at Dora sadly. He really wanted to keep her but it wasn't to be.

He was downcast as they sailed back to London but he didn't try to stop Tiger Lily when she jumped from the boat and ran off as they landed.

She stopped after a short distance and looked back at him, giving a wag of her tail. Peter raised his hand in farewell and then went to collect another pile of dung from the fire-ravaged city. As soon as he got his next wages he was going to buy a dog.

Chapter 12

Tuesday 4 September 1666

'That's it, you're all right,' said a kind voice that Woofer had never heard before. Then Woofer drifted off back to sleep.

Around him was chaos as the fire grew ever stronger. All Cheapside's shops were ablaze and so was Ludgate Hill and Fleet Street. The fire had leapt across the River Fleet and was heading towards the wealthier West End and the royal residences.

The little dog heard another voice and his stub of a tail twitched in recognition. It was the voice of the king but he was too weary to lift his head from the blanket in the cart where he was lying, to see His Majesty on his horse.

'Why haven't these houses been taken down?' the king demanded. 'Don't you understand that they're in the direct line of the fire and will feed its greedy flames.'

'But our homes . . .' protested an old man.

'Where will we live?' asked a woman.

'You'll be recompensed,' said the king.

'How do we know?'

'Because I'm your king and I'm telling you so.'

The king urged his horse onwards through the throng of people and did not see Woofer lying in the cart among all the other carts full of people's possessions.

Woofer woke up again when the cart stopped at a house in Seething Lane.

'We're back, Mr Pepys,' called the boy who'd been pushing the cart. 'All your valuables are now safe at Bethnal Green.'

'Not *all* of my valuables, Will,' Mr Pepys told him. 'There's still my wine and cheese to be buried in the garden.'

He looked in the cart.

'Why do you now have a small dog with you?'

'Couldn't leave him behind, Mr Pepys. He nearly drowned when the boat struck him on its way back from delivering your stuff.'

Mr Pepys sighed. 'And I suppose I'm to feed and water every waif and stray.'

'He can't eat much,' Will said cheekily. 'He's only little.'

'Well, take the cart back now. It was only lent to us for the trip.'

'Ah, but he's asleep again,' Will replied as Woofer snored. 'Wouldn't be right to disturb him.'

Mr Pepys sighed. 'I'm going to fetch the wine and cheese for burial,' he said as he went back inside the house.

Will left Woofer sleeping while he went to the kitchen to have some food.

When the terrier woke again the sun was high overhead and he felt much better.

'Dig deep,' Mr Pepys told Will, who was holding a shovel, and he pointed at a spot in the garden. 'The deeper the cheese and wine are buried, the safer they'll be from the fire.'

'Right you are, Mr Pepys.'

Woofer sat up and watched as Will dug deep into the flower beds and then lifted the soft earth and shook it off the shovel to make a small mound.

The little dog tilted his head to one side and wagged his tail-stub as Will did the same thing again and again.

Finally it was too much for Woofer to resist. He jumped out of the cart and raced over to join in. For once he wasn't in trouble as his paws scrabbled in the soil.

'That's it, dog,' Will said. 'Keep going. Good dog! I knew I was right to rescue you from the river.'

Woofer's tail-stub wagged with excitement as he dug in the dry brown mud. His face and paws and back were soon covered in soil.

'What's that dog doing?'

'He's helping, Mr Pepys,' Will told him. 'Helping to save your precious goods. Right good at digging he is too.'

'That's deep enough. These bottles there. Move over, dog. That hole's deep enough for two more,' declared Mr Pepys, who was supervising the excavation.

Woofer looked at the hole that was now being filled in by Will. He hadn't finished digging there yet!

'What's keeping the maid with my last block of cheese?' Mr Pepys said, and he hurried back into the house to find out.

'I'd say he deserves a bone for all his effort,' Will said, when Mr Pepys came back.

'Right.'

When the refreshments were brought out Woofer gulped down the water and chewed on a bone while Will swallowed two cups of ale and some bread and cheese.

'Reckon your goods are safe from the fire now, Mr Pepys,' he said.

'Yes,' Mr Pepys agreed. 'Thanks in part to this fine little dog.' And he gave Woofer a pat.

The day was almost over and Tiger Lily lay in the doorway of Old St Paul's Church as people carried books inside for safekeeping. But even here the fire found her.

As the church began to burn, the pages in the books burned too and Tiger Lily's fur was covered in paper ash like snow.

Desperate to get away from the flames, Tiger Lily set off along the street. The next moment she yelped and ran into an open doorway to escape the hot stones that came flying down the street towards her.

A thin man with white hair ran into the doorway for protection too.

Tiger Lily looked up at him and whimpered with fear.

'What's a poor wee dog like you doing out here all alone?' the man said, crouching down beside her and giving Tiger Lily a stroke as they waited for the stones to stop flying. 'This is no place for man or beast. Especially one who must belong to someone of importance,' he added, noting her long tail. 'But there's no time to find out who that might be now.'

'John? John Evelyn? What on earth are you doing out here in this? You could have been killed,' said one of the churchwardens as he came down the street, supervising the men carrying buckets of water, fire hooks and squirts to fight the fire.

'I was on my way to the hospital to check on the wounded when I was stopped by this tragedy,' the man replied.

Tiger Lily came out from behind him and looked up at the churchwarden.

'I didn't know you had a dog, John,' he said, giving Tiger Lily a bit of his suppertime pie, which she wolfed down hungrily.

'It's not my dog,' John Evelyn started to say, but the churchwarden was already striding off towards the church with the fire fighters.

Tiger Lily's tummy rumbled. The pie made her think of all the good things she'd had to eat at the palace and she knew where she needed to be. Tiger Lily ran back down towards the river as quickly as she could, because the river led to home.

In Seething Lane, all the digging he'd done made Woofer think of George and he let out a sad whine because he'd never been away from George for so long before.

He trotted out of the garden while Will was taking the cart back to the man Mr Pepys had borrowed it from.

By the time Will got back Woofer was doggedly making his way towards the riverbank; back to George, back to the palace, his home.

The cobblestones were hot beneath his paws and the smoke was thicker than a mist and made it difficult to see. But he was determined to get back to George now and nothing would stop him.

Mostly he kept his head down, looking at the ground; less smoke seemed to catch in his throat that way.

The little terrier wasn't far from the Tower in Tower Street when he saw a dog in front of him and for a brief second it raised its long tail. Woofer's heart quickened, as did his step. But the smoke all around stopped him from picking up a clear scent and he was too exhausted to run, and still only just recovering from the blow to his head.

The other dog disappeared into the smoke and although Woofer's throat was raw he gave one of his distinctive woofs, then looked back down at the cobblestones as he trotted on. A moment later he heard a bark in reply and lifted his head. Coming through the smoke, running towards him as if her life depended on it, was Tiger Lily.

Tiger Lily couldn't believe that she'd found her friend at last and her tail lifted in a joyous wag as she raced through the smoke-filled air towards Woofer. Her coat was no longer cream and tan but soot-blackened grey.

Woofer's tail-stub had never wagged so hard in its life and he made happy little whimpering sounds as he ran towards her.

Neither of them saw the men placing the gunpowder, then stepping back once the fuse was lit.

The explosion threw the dogs to opposite ends of the street like leaves, the sound of it ringing in their ears.

The men who'd detonated the blast slapped each other on the back as the lions, elephants, great apes and bears in the king's zoo at the Tower roared and howled in terror.

'We've just helped to stop the fire!' the men said to each other. 'It can't keep going if there's nothing to burn in its path.'

Other firebreaks like it had been lit around the city, blowing up buildings in the fire's path so it couldn't jump from one to another.

But as the wind dropped and the fire's frenzy gradually abated, one of the dogs crawled slowly and painfully on its belly through the smoke-filled air across the cobblestones towards the other.

The men who'd set off the explosion didn't notice a small dog lying on the ground, not moving, and they were walking away when the other dog threw back its head and howled into the sky.

Chapter 13

Teeth and Claws led George and Annie through the grey fog of smoke, thick dust, fine ash and steam. There were explosions all around them as more houses were blown up and others collapsed and crashed to the ground, weakened by the fire.

In some streets they went down, the flames were now under control but the stones and rubble were so hot that the soles of their shoes and the dogs' paw pads were burnt as they walked along them. The brindle-coloured fur of Teeth and Claws was now a soft grey because of all the dust and they looked almost like ghost dogs. George glanced over at Annie. She resembled a ghost too, apart from her eyes.

So many buildings had been destroyed that London was almost unrecognizable and the thick, strange-smelling and cough-inducing air made detecting the scent of Woofer and Tiger Lily almost impossible for Teeth and Claws. Their trot turned to a walk until finally they stopped.

Claws looked up at George and gave a whine as Teeth lay down on the hot cobblestones, too exhausted to care whether they singed his fur or not.

George bit his cracked lip. It had been hours since they'd had anything to drink and his mouth felt as dry as the dust that surrounded them. It was hopeless. They'd never find Woofer and Tiger Lily.

But just as George was thinking this, Teeth suddenly jumped up and ran over to a large pile of debris from one of the houses that had been pulled down to make a firebreak. Claws followed close behind him.

'Do you think they've picked up the scent again?' Annie said as the dogs started pawing at a particular spot. George didn't know but they both went to see what the dogs were doing.

Claws looked up at him and gave a bark.

'What is it, Claws?' George asked as they watched the dogs digging and pawing.

'Do you think someone's under it? They couldn't still be alive, could they?' Annie said doubtfully.

'I don't see how anyone could be alive under all that,' George replied. 'Come on, Teeth. This way, Claws!'

But the dogs wouldn't leave the spot. They barked and whined as they dug away at the ruins of the wattle and daub building.

Passers-by gathered to see what was going on and suddenly George heard a small cry coming from under the rubble.

'There's someone down there and they're alive!' he cried.

The bystanders started to help the dogs by moving the wood and stones.

'Careful now, not too fast or it could all cave in,' warned a man wearing a battered hat.

Ten minutes later two small children and their mother were pulled out. They'd been safe but stuck beneath two heavy oak timbers that had fallen across each other, leaving a narrow space for them to crawl into when the building came tumbling down.

'The house collapsed around us,' the mother said. 'We've been under there all night. I kept calling and calling for help and had just about given up when it finally came.'

'You and your children are lucky to be alive,' the man in the battered hat told her. 'You've got those two dogs over there to thank most of all, as well as this young man.'

Annie and the two children were stroking Teeth and Claws.

'Thank you,' the mother said to George.

'They're good dogs,' he told her, 'but I didn't know they could do that.'

Teeth and Claws had spent most of their lives in the turnspit wheel and only now, in this crisis, was he seeing just how amazing they were.

'We're heading to Moorfields,' the man in the hat told the children's mother, and she nodded. That was where most people were going.

Teeth and Claws watched as the now homeless family grabbed whatever belongings they could find and followed the throng heading towards the city wall. Some of the crowd pulled or pushed handcarts containing all their remaining possessions. Everyone was loaded down with as much as they could carry on their backs. They didn't talk much as they walked. The expressions on their tired grimy faces were sometimes bewildered and tearful, but more often than not there was also a determination about them. They gritted their teeth as they trudged on, not knowing what was to become of them now.

Annie gave Teeth and Claws the rope toy to sniff again and this time Claws held it in his mouth as the dogs led them onwards past piles of rubble that shifted and slid as they carefully edged their way along them.

The hard biscuits she'd been trying to ration were almost gone now but Annie broke one into small pieces and gave them to the dogs. Teeth and Claws – briefly dropping the rope toy – gobbled the crumbs down.

They were all hungry and exhausted but most of all they were desperately thirsty.

George didn't want to say out loud what he'd been thinking all day, because it was too terrible to contemplate, but if they didn't find

Woofer and Tiger Lily soon he feared they might never find them. What chance did they have in this grey, sooty, smoke-filled desolation?

Annie looked up at the yellow-tinged sky. 'If only it would rain,' she said. 'Just rain.'

But although there was lots of smoke there wasn't a cloud in the sky.

George couldn't bear to think about poor Woofer and Tiger Lily, alone and frightened. They didn't even know anyone was searching for them.

As they approached the river again Teeth and Claws' tail-stubs started to wag. Claws gave an excited whine and the next moment the two dogs broke into a run, and George and Annie grinned at each other and ran after them.

George's heart was thumping hard. He was gasping for air. Maybe, just maybe they were going to find Woofer and Tiger Lily at last.

But then, close to Tower Street, Teeth and Claws suddenly stopped. Teeth sniffed at the ground, pawed at it and whined. Then he looked up at George and barked.

George stared down at the blood on the ground where Teeth was pawing and his heart sank. He didn't know whose blood it was but he feared the worst when Claws lifted his head to the sky and howled.

'Do you think the blood . . .' Annie started to say.

But George shook his head. He didn't want to talk about it. He wouldn't give up hope.

'Find,' George told the dogs. 'Find!'

And Teeth and Claws put their noses to the ground and sniffed. Their way towards London Bridge was blocked and they had to turn back, finding themselves close to where George had first met Woofer, seven months ago.

He remembered holding the terrier in his arms on the ice, the smell of his puppiness and the fragility of his furry little body.

‘Where are you, Woofer?’ George murmured as Teeth and Claws turned away from the river and walked on and on through the night. ‘He’s a tough little dog,’ he told Annie. ‘If anyone can make it he can and as for Tiger Lily, well, when she wants something she won’t stop until she gets it.’

Annie smiled and brushed away a tear as George told her about Tiger Lily coming all the way down the steep stairs from the king’s apartments to the kitchen when she was just a few months old.

Telling Annie stories about the puppies made him feel more hopeful but he couldn’t rid his mind of that blood on the ground.

Finally, at dawn, they reached the Moor Gate in the city wall that led to Moorfields.

‘Oh no,’ Annie gasped.

Before them, as far as the eye could see, were thousands and thousands and thousands of people, covered in the same grey dust that covered them.

Teeth had the rope toy in his mouth now. Claws, George and Annie followed him as he trotted on into the crowds.

Most of the people were lying down, exhausted by the horror of it all. Many of them looked like they were asleep, not wanting to wake up and discover that the nightmare they'd been having was actually real.

They lay huddled together for comfort, their heads resting on their sacks of belongings, still wearing the clothes they'd run away from their homes in. Some of their garments were burnt, many of them tattered and torn, all of them smelling of smoke.

George, Annie and the dogs stepped over outstretched arms and legs of sleepers. Annie raised her hand to her eyes as she looked out at the sea of people ahead of them. She couldn't see where it ended – it seemed to go on forever.

George felt as though he could fall asleep right where he stood. But he forced his feet to keep moving, one in front of the other, as the dogs walked ahead of them. Impossible as it now seemed, they had to keep looking for Woofer and Tiger Lily. They couldn't give up on them.

As they made their way through the crowds more people started to wake up.

'What've you got those dogs for?' a man wanted to know.

'These aren't my dogs. They belong to the king and they work in his kitchen,' George said.

'Then why aren't they with him now?'

'We're looking for two other dogs that belong to the king,' Annie replied. 'One spaniel and one terrier. Have you seen them?'

But no one had.

Lots of families and friends had become separated in the panic of the fire and were searching for each other. People wandered past, looking dazed. Most had lost everything.

'How are we supposed to survive?' they asked each other.

Lost children wandered among the vast crowds looking for their relatives. A boy aged about four stopped in front of them and Claws nuzzled his hand for stroke.

'Have you seen my mother?' the boy asked Annie and George as he patted Claws. His eyes were red-rimmed from crying and tiredness and the smoke. The dust made his hair look as grey as an old man's.

George shook his head. 'What's your name?' he asked.

'Henry,' the boy replied as he went with them through the vast crowd, looking desperately from side to side for his mother as his hand rested on the dog's back.

More than food, they still needed a drink and George gratefully took a jug of barley water that some soldiers were handing out. George, Annie and Henry took it in turns to gulp and gulp. The boiled-grain water had never tasted so good. Teeth and Claws needed to quench their thirst too and George and Annie poured barley water into their cupped hands for the dogs to lap but made sure any drips fell back into the jug. They didn't know when more would be coming and didn't want to waste a drop.

George wiped his mouth on his sleeve. How were they supposed to find Woofer and Tiger Lily among so many sad, weary, desperate people?

'We're all doomed,' George heard one woman say to another. 'The comet in January foretold that it was coming.'

'What was coming?' the other woman asked her.

'Judgement Day.'

'Henry!' a woman shouted as she ran towards them, pushing through the crowd, stumbling and almost falling but recovering. 'Henry!'

And then Henry saw her and ran to his mother and she scooped the little boy up in her arms and hugged him tight.

'I thought I'd lost you forever,' she cried, Henry clinging to her as if he'd never let go. 'Thank you,' she said to George and Annie as they and the dogs walked on.

'How are we ever going to find two small dogs among all these people?' Annie said, an hour later.

'It's impossible,' George said, but they carried on through the mass of people anyway and eventually passed out of Moorfields and further into Finsbury Fields, the crowd thinning out a little towards the wooded end.

As they walked they kept asking people if anyone had seen a spaniel and a terrier but everyone just shook their weary heads. They kept on walking and asking anyway. They couldn't give up on finding Woofer and Tiger Lily.

Finally they came across a girl sharing a tattered blanket with her mother, who said she'd seen two small dogs.

'One of them was bleeding,' she added, pointing towards the trees.

George, Annie, Teeth and Claws ran for all they were worth.

Chapter 14

The raggedy cat sat on a low branch, her tail twitching every now and again as she watched the spaniel in the stream. Tiger Lily's celebrated capture of the small trout at Tunbridge in July had just been for sport; now she had to catch fish for herself and Woofer to eat. She caught some for the raggedy cat too although the cat was more than able to fend for herself.

Tiger Lily waited for a fish to swim past in the dappled light of the water and then she pounced. The raggedy cat stretched and leapt down from the tree to join Woofer, who was lying beneath it.

The wound in Woofer's side where the debris from the explosion had hit him was infected, and he lay on his other side, panting. Every now and then he cried out or whimpered in pain.

Tiger Lily laid the fish next to him but Woofer didn't even seem to know it was there. A rat, caught earlier for him by the raggedy cat, lay untouched close by.

Tiger Lily pushed the trout closer to Woofer with her nose but Woofer still didn't eat. Tiger Lily curled up next to her friend and slept.

As she dreamt her paws twitched at the memory of the night of the explosion.

Woofer's blood on the ground, so much blood, but she knew they had to get away, somewhere safe. She'd pushed and pawed at him and finally he'd stood up and, leaning on her for support, had staggered through the night streets.

They wouldn't have made it without the raggedy cat, who'd appeared out of the smoke and helped to bear the weight of the little dog from the other side.

When Woofer was about to lie down and not go any further, they pushed him on. Tiger Lily didn't trust the people around them any more. People who'd tried to put her in a cage, people who'd hurt Woofer, and so she led them as far away from everyone as she could. But even here wasn't far enough.

Her sleep was disturbed by the sound of someone calling her friend's name.

'Woofer!' a voice cried, and Tiger Lily opened her eyes to see George, Teeth, Claws and Annie standing there.

The raggedy cat hissed at them and scampered back into the tree but Tiger Lily jumped up and wagged her tail at Teeth and Claws as the turnspit dogs wagged their tail-stubs back at her. Teeth dropped the rope toy that he'd been carrying at Tiger Lily's feet. They'd found their friends at last.

Tiger Lily licked Annie's hand over and over as Annie stroked her, while George knelt down beside Woofer.

'It's all right,' he told the little dog. 'I'm here and you're safe now.'

Woofer looked up at him and whimpered.

George bit his bottom lip as he looked at Woofer's wound. It needed treatment – and fast. Without it the puppy would die.

He went to the stream and soaked the apron Annie had given him in clean water and then came back to wash Woofer's wound.

Woofer whined and put his paw out to stop him but it had to be done and George was as gentle as he could be.

In the distance, too far away for George and Annie to hear but not too far for a dog's sensitive ears, Tiger Lily heard a familiar voice. She turned her head towards the sound and gave a yap. But George was too busy seeing to Woofer to pay her any attention and Annie was down at the stream with Teeth and Claws, who were having a long drink.

The raggedy cat was still up in the branches of the tree, refusing to come down.

Tiger Lily gazed in the direction of the noise again. It was the sound of strokes and food and play, soft cushions and kind words. It was the sound of home.

'*I desire you all to take no more alarm . . .*'

She looked at Woofer, safe now with George, and whimpered, looked towards the sound of the voice and whined, and the next moment she was gone, racing across the late-summer fields, weaving in and out of the homeless people that surrounded him until she reached the tall man on the horse.

'Tiger Lily!' the king cried, and he climbed off his horse as the tan and cream puppy, her coat still damp from the stream, ran into his arms.

‘I thought I’d lost you forever, little one,’ he said, hugging her to him.

Tiger Lily’s little pink tongue licked and licked his face.

‘Time we were departing,’ he said at last and stood up. But Tiger Lily squirmed in his arms and then jumped from them, racing back towards the wooded area.

The king found George tending a shivering Woofer while Annie sat with Teeth and Claws. He didn’t even notice the raggedy cat up in the branches of the tree.

‘Woofer’s too badly injured to walk,’ George said as Tiger Lily lay down next to her friend and nuzzled him with her nose.

‘Well then he shall ride,’ said the king. ‘There’s room enough on my horse for two small dogs and the Court physician shall tend to his needs.’ He looked over at Teeth and Claws. ‘I see you now have many dogs,’ he said.

'They're turnspit dogs from the palace kitchen, sir,' George told him. 'Without Teeth and Claws we'd never have found Tiger Lily and Woofer. They tracked their scent through the city.'

'How amazing,' the king agreed. 'I should very much like to see their tracking skills. They should be playfellows for the royal dogs from now on, as should dear Woofer once he's fully recovered.'

George looked over at Annie. Her head was down and in front of the king she was suddenly very shy, not at all like her usual self.

'Annie made the biscuits that the royal dogs like so much, sir,' George said.

'Did she indeed?' the king remarked.

Annie, not sure what she was supposed to do in the presence of such greatness, jumped up, curtsied and blushed. Instinctively she smoothed down her hair, at the same time attempting to say that yes, indeed, she was Annie, and what an honour it was to speak to His Majesty. But no words would come out of her mouth and she could only open and close it silently.

'I've often thought we should employ a cook at the palace for the royal dogs,' said the king as he took off his cloak and wrapped Woofer in it.

George smiled. Woofer would be OK now. But then he had another thought. If Teeth and Claws were to be royal playfellows and Annie the royal dog chef, then what about him?

The king must have been a mind reader because he answered George's question before George had even asked it.

'And you, George, are now Assistant Keeper of the Palace Dogs, both royal and otherwise. James Jack would have no one else for the role,' he said as he carried Woofer to his horse.

Woofer weakly wagged his stub of a tail and George couldn't think of anything that he would like more than to work with the dogs.

'Thank you, Your Majesty,' he said, his eyes shining. Gran would never have believed it. Thinking of her made him sad but then he imagined her busily making pottage up in heaven and he didn't feel sad any more.

'Make haste to return. I think you'll find things a little different in the palace kitchen where you used to work,' said the king as he rode off with Woofer and Tiger Lily.

When George, Teeth, Claws and Annie got back to the palace kitchen, followed by the raggedy cat, there was a sound coming from it that George had never heard in there before – Geese; six of them, all looking quite at home.

The goose in the turnspit wheel didn't seem to mind the work at all as it strutted round and round. In fact the bird looked quite proud of its new role.

'They've got wood tar and sand on their feet. That's how they're protected when they walk to

Nottingham Goose Fair from all over the country. It gives their feet more of a grip when walking in the wheel too,' a man with thick sandy-coloured locks told George and Annie. For a moment the hair confused George but then Humphrey lifted it off like a hat and he realized it was a wig.

'You're back!' George cried, throwing his arms round his friend.

'Of course I am. It doesn't take that long to get to Nottingham and back.'

'So that's where you went?'

'But the geese didn't have to walk here from Nottingham, did they?' Annie asked him.

'Oh no,' Humphrey laughed. 'They rode home in style in the carriage with me!' He turned back to George. 'Didn't anyone tell you I was going there to buy geese to work the turnspit wheel?'

George shook his head.

'Honestly, sometimes I think you and I are the only ones with any brains around here.'

'They were probably too scared of Master Vogel,' George laughed. He was glad the chef had gone now.

'Yes. Can't say I'm sad to see the back of him either,' said Humphrey.

Leopold, the Archduke of Austria, had commanded him home and everyone was happy to see him leave.

Teeth and Claws went to sniff 'hello' to the five geese that weren't in the wheel but when the birds hissed at them they quickly retreated.

Tiger Lily came racing into the kitchen wagging her tail and as George followed her up the stairs, the cat slipped into the kitchen, ran over to Old Peg on her stool and jumped up on to her lap.

'Hello, cat,' the old lady said, and she stroked her until the ragged-tailed cat purred.

In an anteroom off the king's apartments Woofer had now been treated for his injuries and was fast asleep. A silver bowl of water and some tasty snacks had been set down beside him.

Once Woofer was well enough, George took him for short walks in the Privy Garden and, as he got stronger, for longer ones in St James's Park.

Woofer still wasn't too sure about the large pelicans over on Duck Island but he wasn't scared of the thirty chickens that had now made their home in the park and he wagged his tail at the baby goats.

The king gave Woofer's sapphire collar back to him. 'It was always his to keep,' he said.

'He does look very smart in it, Your Majesty,' George grinned.

A few months later there was great excitement in the palace when Tiger Lily gave birth to three puppies. Three perfect mixtures of Tiger Lily and Woofer mewled and snuffled as their mum licked them and Woofer wagged the stub of his tail.

For the first few weeks their eyes and ears were closed but once they opened, the puppies were up and about and full of life. They tumbled over each other, exploring the room they'd been born in and crunching up the biscuits Annie made especially for them with their sharp little puppy teeth. Annie was more than happy with her new customers and loved working in Humphrey's kitchen.

The puppies caused laughter and havoc wherever they went and George, Annie and James Jack were kept very busy.

The king's bathtub was a popular place for splashing in and the king's old wigs became favourite chew toys. His Majesty didn't mind a bit. He was too busy organizing food and shelter for his homeless subjects and talking to planners about a new London. A London that would be safer for its people, where there would be less overcrowding and more sanitation.

'We'll rebuild the city,' he said. 'And we'll make it better. A place all people can call home.'

Woofer gave one of his distinctive deep barks.

'Sssh, Woofer,' George said.

But the king only smiled. 'And better for dogs as well, of course,' he added.

Afterword

Researching the Great Fire of London has been fascinating. I'd never have imagined that there used to be frost fairs on the River Thames when it froze over. Or that a small dog had such a crucial role to play in the seventeenth-century kitchen. I am of course indebted to Samuel Pepys and John Evelyn for their diaries of the time that were so enlightening.

The response from children to the idea for this book was very enthusiastic and I hope I have done it justice.

King Charles the Second's love of dogs is well known, but less well known nowadays is the kitchen dog or turnspit as they were known. These short-legged little dogs worked to turn the kitchen wheel that perhaps inspired today's hamster wheels. Sadly the original turnspit dogs died out when they were no longer needed to turn the wheel any more. We do know that Glen Imaal terriers (like Woofer in this book) claim to be their descendants. Some sources say they were related to corgis (like Scraps in this book) and some that it was just any short-legged, long-bodied mixed-breed dog (like Teeth and Claws).

These hard-working little dogs were considered so lowly, little more than kitchen utensils, that no one thought to keep accurate records of them and there are lots of conflicting descriptions of what they looked like. I wish I could have met one of them. I'm sure they'd have loved to play with my dogs and could have been dog-treat taste testers too. Have a look at the end of the book for recipes of a couple of Bella and Freya's favourite treats!

Acknowledgements

Huge thanks as always must go to my wonderful editors Anthea Townsend and Carmen McCulloch, editorial manager Samantha Stanton Stewart, copy-editor Mary O'Riordan and proof-reader Bea McIntyre, cover designer Emily Smyth, and illustrator Richard Jones. On the PR and marketing side there's been brilliant Jessica Farrugia-Sharples, Lucie Sharpe and Hannah Malocco as well as sales champions Tineke Mollemans and Kirsty Bradbury; never forgetting my lovely agent Clare Pearson of Eddison Pearson.

My amazing husband Eric designs my websites, helps with the research for my books, takes fantastic pictures of animals and people, and is the photographer for our local RSPCA. My dogs continue to inspire my writing and bring so much joy to my life. They are the perfect writer's companion. Golden retriever Bella has been coming with me to schools, libraries and festivals, meeting children and showing them her 'helpful' tricks. Little golden retriever puppy Freya will no doubt soon be joining us on our trips.

Dog Treat Recipes

Make sure you ask an adult to help you, especially with the bits involving a hot oven!

The first recipe is very much like the one Annie in the book would have used to make hardtack or ship's biscuits for the sailors back in 1666. My dogs happily crunched them up, but the longer they're left out in the air the harder they get. The sailors would have soaked them to soften them a little before they were eaten, otherwise there would have been a lot of broken teeth! Soaking also got rid of the 'weevils' or maggot larvae from the biscuits. (My dogs probably wouldn't have minded eating those too. ☺)

Ginger Hardtack Biscuits

You will need:

100g flour (any flour except self-raising will do. Do note, however, that some dogs are allergic to wheat)

30ml water

1 tsp of ginger powder

How to make them:

1. Preheat your oven to 180°C or gas mark 4.
2. Mix all the ingredients together in a bowl to make a dough (it should be fairly dry) and knead it with your hands.
3. Roll the dough out until it's roughly a centimeter thick (it doesn't have to be exact) prick holes on both sides of it

with a fork and place on an ungreased baking tray.

4. Pop the tray in the oven and bake for 30 minutes on one side and then flip over and bake for 30 minutes on the other side.
5. Turn off the oven and allow the biscuit to cool inside it (if you can – I couldn't . . .).

When it was still slightly warm I took the biscuit out of the oven and broke it into small pieces. It was already hard, but still breakable, and the bit I tested tasted of ginger – it was definitely edible. An hour later the biscuits were too hard for my teeth, but the dogs crunched them up and a few hours later they were truly hard and lived up to the name of hardtack. I would have tried soaking them for longer as the sailors did to soften them up, but the rest of the pieces had already been eaten by the dogs. The second batch I kept in a glass treat jar and they didn't end up going as hard as those left to air dry, but were still nice and crunchy! ☺

Freya's Ginger Apple Snaps

Our new puppy, Freya, loves apple and so this recipe seemed perfect for her. She also loves raw carrots and pears and either of those could be substituted for the apple.

You will need:

120g rice flour (or you could grind up uncooked rice)
100ml water
1 small apple, grated
1 dsp coconut oil
1 tsp ginger powder

How to make them:

1. Preheat your oven to 180°C, gas mark 4.
2. Combine all the ingredients in a large mixing bowl together and stir. (It will be quite wet but don't worry.)
3. Line a baking tray with greased parchment paper.
4. Press the mixture out on the parchment paper.
5. Bake for 15 minutes. Check if they're done. Keep cooking for up to another 10 minutes if need be. They should feel a bit like a flapjack – crunchy round the edges, softer in the middle. They'll harden up once they cool.

Both biscuits recipes were taste-tested by willing canine volunteers, Bella and Freya.

And the taste-test winner? Well, there really was no contest. Ginger Apple Snaps won hands down! I tasted both too and I have to agree. Ginger Apple Snaps are delicious and stayed crisp and crunchy to the last one in the jar (eaten a few days later ☺).

A PUFFIN BOOK

stories that last a lifetime

Ever wanted a friend who could take you to magical realms, talk to animals or help you survive a shipwreck? Well, you'll find them all in the **A PUFFIN BOOK** collection.

A PUFFIN BOOK will stay with you **forever**. Maybe you'll read it again and again, or perhaps years from now you'll suddenly **remember** the moment it made you **laugh** or **cry** or simply see things **differently**. Adventurers **big** and **small**, rebels out to **change** their world, even a mouse with a **dream** and a spider who can spell – these are the characters who make **stories** that last a **lifetime**.

Whether you love animal tales, war stories or want to know what it was like growing up in a different time and place, the **A PUFFIN BOOK** collection has a story for you – you just need to decide where you want to go next . . .

Tiddles was a ship cat born and raised. He served with the HMS Victorious in the early 1940s as the official 'Captain's Cat' and travelled over 30,000 miles during his naval service.

Fun Fact! It's thought that Tiddles may be one of the reasons why the black cat is considered lucky in Great Britain.

Seconds away from Lekeux being discovered, Pitouchi jumped out of the hole on to a piece of wood nearby. The startled Germans fired twice but luckily Pitouchi was not hit. The Germans, thinking they had mistaken a cat for a man, left the area and Lekeux went back to the Belgian lines with the unharmed cat on his shoulder.

Pitouchi

During the First World War, Lieutenant Lekeux of the Belgian Army had a devoted pet cat called Pitouchi. One time, Lekeux was hiding in a shell hole near the German lines when he heard soldiers approaching. A soldier sensing movement came closer to the shell hole.

Throughout the First World War, cats were a common sight in the trenches and aboard ships, where they hunted mice and rats. They were also embraced as mascots and pets by the soldiers and sailors they served with.

Courageous Cats

He was presented with the Dickin Medal on behalf of all the other animals that served during the First World War.

Fun Fact! Horses like Warrior inspired a children's book and play, *War Horse*, by Michael Morpurgo.

Warrior was often called 'the horse the Germans could not kill'. His rider was General Jack Seely during the First World War and he stuck with him through machine gun fire and falling shells at the Battle of the Somme. Warrior survived his injuries and lived with the Seely family on the Isle of Wight after the war.

The Animal Hero whose story lives on

He flew over four hundred kilometres to deliver the message and his actions saved the lives of two thousand soldiers at the battle of Arnhem.

William of Orange

was a pigeon with the 2nd Parachute Battalion Signals Section during the Second World War. He was awarded the Dickin Medal for the delivery of a message from the Arnhem Airborne Operation in record time in September 1944.

The crew were all rescued and Winkie was awarded the Dickin Medal for her brave efforts.

Fun Fact! The crew held a dinner in Winkie's honour a few days after the rescue.

Winkie was one of the bravest pigeons who served during the Second World War. She saved the crew of a Beaufort Bomber when it crashed into the North Sea. Winkie escaped from the plane and flew 129 miles to Scotland, where the exhausted pigeon alerted the aerodrome to their plight.

More than 100,000 pigeons served Great Britain in the First World War and ninety five per cent of them returned with their messages.

An Unlikely Hero

Tich, a mixed-breed dog, served with the 1st Battalion King's Royal Rifle Corps in North Africa and Italy in the Second World War. She often rode with the battalion on the gun carrier or on the bonnet of a jeep. Tich was severely wounded on a few occasions but refused to leave her post even under heavy attack.

Fun Fact!

He was even given the job of checking that the forest was clear of mines when Britain's Prime Minister, Winston Churchill, came to visit.

Rex was a stray black Labrador who found mines in the Reichswald Forest in 1945. He found so many that platoon commander Lieutenant Peter Norbury described Rex as the bravest dog he had ever seen.

She was able to let the prisoners know when dangerous animals like snakes or tigers were around. Judy was eventually smuggled out of the camp in a rice sack and lived out the rest of her days with Leading Aircraftman Frank Williams – a fellow prisoner of war.

Judy, a brown and white pointer, was captured by the Japanese during World War II and held in a prisoner-of-war camp. She was the only dog to be registered as a prisoner of war during the Second World War.

He became a search and rescue dog and went on to save the lives of over a hundred people.

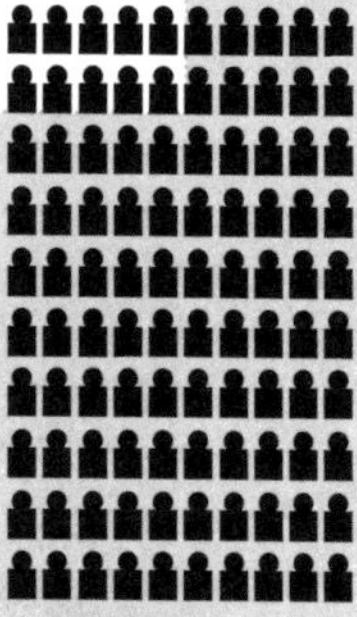

Rip was a mixed-breed terrier found homeless and starving after a bombing raid in 1940.

Prince was an Irish terrier who followed his master from West London to France in 1914. He found him in the trenches at Armiens after attaching himself to some troops who crossed the Channel!

Dogs of War

During the First World War, adverts in newspapers asked for loans of British dogs for use in defence. Within two weeks, the War Office had received an incredible 7,000 offers of dogs. Read on to find out more about dogs in wartime.

Rats was a dog soldier who served with British Army units in Northern Ireland during the Troubles and took part in patrols, car chases and even helicopter flights. He was shot at and lost several inches of his tail in an explosion!

Fun Fact! Rats was so well loved that the army gave him a parade when he retired.

Peggy the mongrel was so heroic that she was awarded a special collar. She dug a hole in the debris of her house after a bomb fell on it to allow her owner's baby to breathe. Everyone who lived there was saved thanks to Peggy!

Hero Pups!

This little book of animal heroes will tell you all about some incredible furry and feathery friends. Find out about brave dogs, heroic horses, courageous cats and even valiant pigeons!

megan rix

Little Book of Animal Heroes

PUFFIN

PFC Hammer: Even in recent years, a good mouser is still cherished. This handy cat moved in with the troops of a US Army unit in Iraq in 2004, killing and chasing away mice that would have eaten the soldiers' food stores. The men were so grateful for Hammer's hard work and affection towards them that they made him an honorary member of their unit. He now lives in Colorado with his old comrade, Staff Sergeant Rick Bousfield.

PUFFIN BOOKS
UK | USA | Canada | Ireland | Australia
India | New Zealand | South Africa

Puffin Books is part of the Penguin Random House group of companies whose addresses can be found at global.penguinrandomhouse.com.

www.penguin.co.uk www.puffin.co.uk www.ladybird.co.uk

Penguin Random House UK

First published 2017
001

Printed in Italy

A CIP catalogue record for this book is available from the British Library

ISBN: 978-0-141-38656-0